The Woman Who Ran AIIMS

The Woman Who Ran AIIMS

The Memoirs of a Medical Pioneer

Sneh Bhargava

juggernaut

JUGGERNAUT BOOKS
C-I-128, First Floor, Sangam Vihar, Near Holi Chowk,
New Delhi 110080, India

First published by Juggernaut Books 2025

Copyright © Sneh Bhargava 2025

10 9 8 7 6 5 4 3 2 1

P-ISBN: 9789353457235
E-ISBN: 9789353455262

The views and opinions expressed in this book are the author's own. The facts contained herein were reported to be true as on the date of publication by the author to the publishers of the book, and the publishers are not in any way liable for their accuracy or veracity.

All rights reserved. No part of this publication may be reproduced, transmitted, or stored in a retrieval system in any form or by any means without the written permission of the publisher.

Typeset in Adobe Caslon Pro by R. Ajith Kumar, Noida

Printed at Replika Press Pvt. Ltd.

For my parents
My husband – Amar
My children – Anjulika and Sandeep
My siblings – the Taneja siblings

Contents

Author's Note ix
Foreword xv

1. My First Day as Director of AIIMS 1
2. Family, Childhood and Partition 14
3. Lady Hardinge Medical College 29
4. Studies in Post-Empire England 45
5. The Start of My Career in Radiology and My Married Life 57
6. Fighting for Respect for Radiology at AIIMS 72
7. Turning to the West for the Best Technology 100
8. Building Up the Radiology Department Against the Cynics 110
9. Director of AIIMS 121
10. VIP Tales 159
11. Life Is Like Riding a Bicycle. To Keep Your Balance, You Must Keep Moving 170
12. All About Doctors 188

Appendix A: My Research and Publications 200
Appendix B: Awards and Honours 225
Appendix C: How Others Saw Me 229

Author's Note

I was inspired to write my memoir at the age of 94 by an Abraham Lincoln quote: 'In the end, it's not the years in your life that count, it's the life in your years.' I retired from the All India Institute of Medical Sciences (AIIMS) in my sixtieth year, the only woman director in the institute's history, and had no thought of writing anything. I felt I had not done anything very special, only discharged my duties passionately and created a brand that I hoped would grow stronger and maintain its position as the best hospital in the country. Throughout my career as a doctor, both before and after AIIMS, my motivating force was to honour the education that my parents had made sacrifices for – an education that was the best that money could buy – and to repay the trust they had placed in my abilities. My parents provided me with a Western education and Eastern values, and I faced no gender bias from them at any stage of my life. It fills me with admiration to think of how fiercely forward-looking and progressive they were despite the deeply patriarchal society they lived in during the early decades of the twentieth century.

Over the years, dear friends from the medical profession urged me to write about my career and experiences. They all offered to help me with the task and kept encouraging me, but ultimately, I had to have the will and desire to recollect my life's journey, and it was then that Abraham Lincoln's remark struck me.

One of the main reasons for my reluctance was my failure to keep a diary or notes on my long and active life, a failure that was perhaps influenced by one of my father's favourite sayings: *Neki karo aur kuein me daalo*, which means 'do good and forget about it; do not expect any reward'. What I did have, however, was a notebook that I always kept in the pocket of my white coat, titled 'Mistaken Diagnosis', in which I religiously took detailed notes as to why I made a particular mistake. I shared these experiences with my students so that they could learn as much from them as I had, so that the mistakes were never repeated. But even here, I wondered why anyone would be interested in reading about my mistakes given that technology had moved forward so much from when I started down the untrodden path of diagnostics radiology in India. For the uninitiated, this is a medical speciality that uses imaging to create pictures of the inside of the body to help diagnose illnesses.

By 1990, I had retired from AIIMS. A century had passed since the discovery of X-rays by Röntgen in 1895, and that year, I chaired a national exhibition celebrating radiology decade by decade, chronicling its journey from the early days when X-rays were used to detect tumours that the eye could not see to diagnosing the actual molecules in those tumours by magnetic resonance imaging (MRI). My friends kept pushing me to write my memoir, but I was just too busy. After my retirement from AIIMS, I was involved in teaching and patient care at two hospitals. I have never had an idle day in my life, right into my 90s. I had no time to pick up my pen. Then Covid-19 struck and enforced leisure on me when the government ordered senior citizens to stay at home. As a super-senior citizen, I was forced to comply, even though I was healthy and active, but it was this enforced period of inactivity that finally prompted me to put pen to paper and record all the juggling and balancing involved in my trinity of responsibilities – teaching, research and patient care, and as a daughter, sister, wife and mother. As director of AIIMS, I had an even larger canvas to cover, which involved dealing with politicians. I had the pleasure of dealing with nine politicians as health ministers and five secretaries in my six-year tenure.

My husband Amar Nath and my family gave me all the support I needed at all times, without me ever having to ask for it. At times, nothing was as important as wearing a mother's cap, and at others, work took precedence owing to the oath I had taken, like many of my generation, to serve society to the best of my ability. As I started writing, I realized I had a story about how I had built up the radiodiagnosis department at AIIMS to be one of the best – if not the best – in the country. This guided and inspired many others to raise their standards. To my great pride, I was considered one of the pillars of the team that built AIIMS as an institution that worked for India's poor. My time at AIIMS was a time of constraints and limited funds and, to put it bluntly, of gross neglect of the health sector. From the 1950s till the 1990s, the health budget allocated for patient care and education was only 0.9 per cent of India's GDP, and the bureaucracy seemed to resent giving even that tiny sum. Contrast this with the World Health Organization's (WHO's) recommendation that health should represent 9–13 per cent of the GDP. We could only plead with the powers that be, and I spared no effort in doing so and then making the most of what I managed to prise out of them. My goal was to train the next generation, creating health manpower for the nation because our future depended on it.

As director of AIIMS, my job was to expand and develop teaching, research and patient care, which was the responsibility that Parliament had entrusted to us. I have tried in my memoir to illustrate how I provided leadership, both in the radiology department and as director of this institution. The obstacles kept arising, I kept overcoming them and the institution kept growing. It gives me great pride to hear that generations of students regard the years of my directorship from 1984 to 1990 as a 'golden period'.

All I can say without the slightest hesitation is that I endeavoured to discharge my duty with dedication and passion. I leave it to the reader to judge my contribution.

I would like to thank my partners – they are far too numerous to name – in this difficult but rewarding journey and urge the generations to come to remember that there will be twists and turns in your career, but there is always room at the top.

Lastly, I have no words to express my gratitude to my faithful and dedicated secretary, Tara Datt Phulara, for the devotion and passion with which he has diligently captured my memories electronically while meticulously performing all the other tasks of managing my office efficiently.

This is not a book for scholars or researchers but for those who want to bring equity in education, research and healthcare to millions of our people so that India can have a healthy workforce.

It is a true account of what can be done if you think you can. I will end by endorsing former president Barack Obama's famous words on his election as the first black president of the United States of America (USA): 'Yes, we can.'

Foreword

I deem it a great privilege to have been asked to write a foreword for a memoir by Professor Sneh Bhargava, one of the icons of post-Independence India, who has spent her life pursuing her vision of bringing world-class technology to the poorest of Indians. Sneh is the only woman to hold the highest position of the premier medical institute of the country – director of AIIMS in New Delhi – and remains the only woman to have held that post in AIIMS's long history. She pioneered the advent of radiology in India and is known in the entire medical community for her unparalleled contribution to medicine. It is a contribution that has inspired more than one generation of medical students who looked up to her not only for her expertise but also for her moral integrity, principled conduct, exacting standards and refusal to compromise on patient care. Her tenure at AIIMS left an indelible mark on medicine because she trained and mentored generations of radiologists who went on to work across India to help diagnose illnesses.

Sneh is an icon in the areas of medicine, medical education and medical research. These three pillars were identified by our first prime minister, Jawaharlal Nehru, and promoted by our first health minister, Rajkumari Amrit Kaur, as the ideals for the newly established AIIMS in New Delhi. Sneh fervently made them her life's mission.

It has been a matter of great pride for me to have been counted as one of her friends for over 60 years. Our acquaintance began at Irwin Hospital in the 1950s and progressed as colleagues at AIIMS since 1965, where we worked together on our common goal of making AIIMS a national centre of excellence, particularly in the field of neuroradiology. She took the radiology department of AIIMS when it was nothing and turned it into the best radiology department in the country. We collaborated to develop neuroradiology as one area of her famous radiology department and worked together on professional excellence and research. Some of our publications, on tuberculosis (TB) of the nervous system, for example, are globally recognized.

Sneh's qualities defy easy description because there are so many: outstanding skills as a radiologist; superb administrator who knew how to make a hospital run well; one of the best diagnosticians of her time, head and shoulders above her peers, who could take one look at a plain image and make a diagnosis, outdoing even the clinician; a kind and compassionate person who always held herself – personally and professionally – to a very exacting standard of integrity and probity; and a wonderfully vibrant and vivacious woman who loves life, basks in the affection of a devoted husband, a large family and circle of friends, and never misses an opportunity to dance and party!

Sneh's journey to achieving iconic status can be traced back to her upbringing as a little girl in a highly respected and wealthy family of legal luminaries, deeply imbued with traditional culture, in pre-Independence Punjab. That her parents' thinking was modern comes out clearly in Chapter 2

(Family, Childhood and Partition). Considering the prevailing sociopolitical environment in the country at that time, it is not surprising that Sneh was sent to a boarding school, Sacred Heart Convent in Dalhousie, at the age of five. It is amazing that her parents chose this option in the early 1930s when educating a girl was almost taboo and when many orthodox Indians would not even have thought of sending their sons to a boarding school at this tender age. It was this upbringing with traditional values and exposure to western education that shaped her character and laid the foundation for her spirit of service that emerged later.

There is another aspect of her early childhood that led her to become an empathetic doctor. While playing with dolls (even before she went to school), she was always the 'doctor', a role that was also applied to her hapless younger sister. Clearly, a strong instinct to be a physician stirred in her during these early years. While circumstances prevented her from being a clinician, her success lay in converting her appointment as a specialist in a para-clinical department (radiology) to virtually a clinical department, initially at Irwin Hospital and later at AIIMS. As she writes in this memoir, her goal on joining AIIMS was simply 'to drag radiology from the periphery of medicine to the mainstream where it would be recognized as invaluable because of the role it could play in reaching an accurate diagnosis'.

Let me provide a little potted biography here which only skims the surface of her career. Sneh started her career as an assistant radiologist at Irwin Hospital, Delhi, in 1958, and served as lecturer at Lady Hardinge Hospital and College. She joined AIIMS as an assistant professor of radiology in 1961, taking over as director of AIIMS in 1984, on the day Prime Minister Indira Gandhi was assassinated, until 1990. She served AIIMS for a total 30 years, 6 of them as director. She also had the honour of being the radiologist to the President of India from 1978 to 1990. After her retirement from AIIMS, Sneh remained associated with AIIMS as professor emeritus. Her so-called retirement was no retirement at all. She became even busier, dividing her time between Sitaram Bhartia Institute of Science and Research in the west of the capital as a senior consultant and Dharamshila Narayana Superspeciality Hospital at the other end, in East Delhi, where she was a senior consultant and also head of the department of imaging services. Her frenetically active 'retirement' years make me think of Dylan Thomas's famous line – 'Do not go gentle into that good night, / Old age should burn and rave at close of day; / Rage, rage against the dying of the light.' What is exemplary about her joining these two not-for-profit hospitals is that Sneh forsook the path that many in her position – and with her credentials – would have taken, that is, join a private hospital with a lucrative income. She does not spell out in this memoir why she chose not to, but I think everyone who knows her understands that it would have clashed with the spirit of service that informed her entire career. Instead, a reputed Sitaram Bhartia and a 300-bed Dharamshila Hospital stand today as a testimony to this devotion.

During her career, Sneh trained countless medical students in research in various aspects related to radiology. Among many other pathbreaking ventures, she pioneered the CT and ultrasound investigations in India. Along the way, she found time to serve as chair of the Medical Education Committee of the National Knowledge Commission (NKC) and chair of the Ethics Committee, Medical Council of India (MCI).

I will not list the countless awards and honours Sneh has received as they could fill a small bookshelf. I will instead settle for mentioning just a few. She is the former president of the Indian Radiology and Imaging Association (IRIA). In 2018, she was awarded honorary membership of the Radiological Society of North America – the only radiologist to be so honoured to date. To name only one of the many lifetime awards she has received, Sneh was awarded the Millennium Award 2000 by the IRIA. In 1991, she was awarded the Padma Shri for her distinguished contribution to medicine.

One feature of her personality that makes Sneh stand out is her constant striving to learn about what is new in technology. Prior to joining the radiology department at AIIMS as an assistant professor in 1961, she had decided to upgrade her knowledge of the subject by going to London for a diploma in medical radio diagnosis (DMRD). As a matter of fact, she had hardly any training in radiology prior to this. Here, the memoir recounts many interesting episodes about how Sneh, a colonial 'subject', fared in the land of the colonial 'master', especially as the only female student in the department of radiology at Westminster Hospital. In the two years she spent there, she was exposed to the contemporary professional status of radiology, which was very different from how it was seen in India at the time. At AIIMS, radiologists were seen as so lowly that they were treated as 'photographers' at best and 'back-office workers' at worst. The radiology department had one 500mA X-ray machine and one Odelca camera for miniature chest X-rays. In fact, AIIMS was lagging behind several other institutions in the country. Madras, Vellore and Bombay were far better equipped. Not only was there a paucity of diagnostic equipment, there was hardly any supporting staff.

Yet, by then, the clinical units at AIIMS had been attracting an increasing number of patients and, hence, demands for radiological investigations were growing. It required active strategic efforts to obtain the necessary facilities while resorting to jugaad in the meantime. Gradually, after tireless efforts, persuasion and the support of collaborative clinical departments (especially cardiothoracic and neurology-neurosurgery), Sneh managed to procure state-of-the-art equipment not only from the health budget but also from other sources such as the Rockefeller Foundation and the Swedish International Development Agency. Medical colleagues who worked outside the institute tended to believe that once you become a faculty member at AIIMS, life was a bed of roses and everything was provided on demand. This was far from the truth. Sneh had to craft all manner of strategies and deploy all her wits to justify her requests for the latest equipment by convincing the faceless bureaucrats why it was needed.

It goes without saying that it is not the bricks and mortar or even the quality of the staff that produces excellence but rather the leadership quality of the faculty. Sneh's leadership, based on an unbending insistence on the highest standards of patient care and professional excellence as well as a refusal to settle for anything middling or mediocre (which some people chafed at, unable to understand her absolute insistence on the best, always), created a dynamic atmosphere at AIIMS, which elevated the institute's reputation to hitherto unscaled heights.

As for her personal expertise in radiology, it was the stuff of legend. When they saw her hitting bull's eye after bull's eye in her diagnoses, her colleagues began talking of how she possessed a 'third eye'. She mentions some of these examples of her uncanny ability to see what others could not in the memoir, and I could easily add a whole list of my own but will settle for only two examples.

My brother-in-law had been admitted to another hospital with back pain, and his wife insisted that he should be moved to AIIMS under my care. It was our practice to sit with the radiologist and look at all the X-rays and other investigations. The other doctors and I, all diagnosed a disc prolapse and prepared for surgery. Sneh was on leave at that time. We went ahead and wheeled my brother-in-law into the operating theatre and then found that it was not a disc prolapse but TB of the spine. When Sneh returned, I showed her the various images but did not give her my brother-in-law's medical history. None of it. She took a look at the X-ray from this angle and that angle, and calmly pronounced without any hesitation: 'This is not a disc prolapse. It is TB.' My colleagues and I were stunned. We had been unable to put our finger on the actual ailment despite having far more knowledge of the patient's history and symptoms.

On another occasion, my mother had to be rushed to AIIMS from Allahabad (now Prayagraj) in acute pain. The day she was admitted, she was crying – the pain was so unbearable. The physicians in Allahabad suspected multiple myeloma. The trusted physician I consulted at AIIMS also suspected malignancy and ordered a barium meal test. I showed the result to Sneh. She diagnosed a lump of fat, a benign tumour, to my great relief. I gave my mother medication for the inflamed artery. The next morning, I went to see her in her ward and asked how she was. 'What do you mean, how am I? I'm absolutely fine and I'm ready to go home,' she replied.

Apart from her 'third eye', a personality trait that became legendary was Sneh's emphasis on discipline. Everyone at AIIMS knew this. Everyone was terrified of her. As one of our colleagues once said, 'If Dr Bhargava is on leave, just install a scarecrow of her somewhere, it's enough to make everyone behave.'

In pursuit of her cherished goal to convert radiologists from 'readers of the black-and-white shadows' who were not fully involved in the overall patient care to partners in patient care, Sneh planned regular interaction with clinicians by organizing what she called 'clinico-radiological conferences' with departments such as neurology, neurosurgery, cardiology and cardiothoracic surgery, which were held every day. They were attended by the faculty, residents and staff from the concerned departments, and detailed discussions took place about every patient, taking into account the clinical picture along with all the relevant investigations, in order to arrive at an evidence-based diagnosis. It was this pioneering initiative by Sneh that led to the evolution of subdisciplines under radiology such as neuroradiology, cardiac radiology and paediatric radiology. Some of these later became fully fledged, independent departments awarding super-speciality degrees. Her department at AIIMS stood out because she moved it to the heart of the hospital, and made it part of the crucial decisions made about diseases and how to treat them. Clinicians depended on her opinion.

She encouraged her younger colleagues to specialize in one of the subspecialties besides general radiology. As her successes took root, it helped to fulfil her desire to move radiology from the basement of medicine to the sunlit uplands of mainstream medicine, and turn the radiology department at AIIMS into a lodestar.

Despite a very heavy patient workload, teaching and training responsibilities and the struggle to continuously revolutionize the department of radiology, Sneh did not neglect the third part of AIIMS's raison d'être: research. Between 1962 and 1998, she published 138 scientific papers and eight chapters for books, many for international publications and reputed journals such as the *British Journal of Radiology*, *Australian Radiology*, *Japanese Heart Journal*, *European Journal of Nuclear Medicine* and *Neurosurgery Review*. Some of her findings, particularly those related to lung diseases and brain TB, received global approbation.

The six years of her directorship is a record of how her responsibilities changed and how she discharged them. This required management skills and public relations skills in addition to her will to take the whole institute – not just one department – to greater heights. New departments were established, which included the Centre for Education, the International Clinical Epidemiology Network (INCLEN) programme to strengthen epidemiology, the biotechnology department, the haematology department and the foundations of the emergency department.

Sneh's journey to the pinnacle of her profession has been a joy, an education and an example to all her students. As her friend and colleague, I have enjoyed being by the ringside, watching her climb one peak after another while never altering her personality or morality to fit anyone's demands. Her journey was not easy but she never let obstacles stop her from reaching the top.

I can only conclude by saying that Sneh deserves the gratitude of the millions of people who benefitted from her services, and of her colleagues who enjoyed her ever-willing collaboration and help.

This memoir has many lessons to teach coming generations if Confucius' adage – study the past if you would define the future – holds good.

Dr P.N. Tandon, MS, FRCS
Former Chief of Neuroscience Centre, AIIMS,
Founder and President, National Brain Research Centre, and National Professor

1

My First Day as Director of AIIMS

Could there possibly be a worse way to start the first day at a new job? Here I was, just having been appointed as director of the All India Institute of Medical Sciences, or AIIMS, India's top hospital, by Prime Minister Indira Gandhi against several other strong contenders. There had been much muttering about how a woman could not possibly handle the task of managing the country's premier medical institution to which tens of millions of Indians flocked from every corner of the country to be healed. As India's first female prime minister, Mrs Gandhi had refused to countenance the argument that a woman was incapable of handling this important post and had instead chosen to let my 24 years of service to the institution, most recently as head of radiology, speak for itself. I was the first female director of AIIMS, and so far, the only one in its history.

Now, on the morning of 31 October 1984, as I stood in the corridor of the ground floor, a few feet away, in the casualty department, lay Mrs Gandhi on a gurney, lifeless. Somewhere in the remote periphery of my consciousness, I registered that the gurney did not even have a bed sheet over it. The cold metal against the skin would have made any patient wince.

Earlier, at 9 a.m., I had been in my office in the radiology department discussing some cases on what I presumed would be a fairly routine first day as director. In fact, the pro forma meeting confirming me as director was underway at that time. A radiographer burst through the door, his white coat flying.

'Come quickly, Madam!' he screamed. 'The prime minister is in casualty! Quickly. I saw Dr Safaya (Dr A.N. Safaya, the medical superintendent) running to her too.'

Knowing hospital protocol, it was unthinkable that a prime minister could come to the hospital without prior notice. I frowned, sensing something was terribly amiss. The panic on the radiographer's face was so wild, I rose to walk quickly to the casualty department, which was only a short distance from my office, to see what the uproar was about.

As I entered through the swing doors, I heard loud wailing. Mrs Gandhi's personal secretary R.K. Dhawan and her political advisor Makhan Lal Fotedar wept. I walked past them to the staff at the desk and saw her. In the confusion of the moment, I had no idea how many other patients were in the casualty ward and what they could see. Mrs Gandhi's daughter-in-law, Sonia Gandhi, was also there. The only words she managed to say were, 'She has been shot', before breaking down. Some resident doctors stood in a huddle, in a state of shock. I saw the signature grey streak in her black hair and the pronounced aquiline nose. Mrs Gandhi's saffron-coloured sari was soaked in blood. Dhawan and Fotedar moved outside into the anteroom. Within a minute, senior surgeons Dr P. Venugopal and Dr M.M. Kapur were at my side to examine her, having been pulled out of the operating theatre to come to casualty.

'What can we do for her?' I asked. She had no pulse. Dr Venugopal suggested putting Mrs Gandhi on the heart-lung machine in the operating theatre to switch off the functioning of her heart and lungs while the doctors could see if they could revive her. 'What are we waiting for? Let's go,' I said, asking Dr Safaya to run down the corridor and hold the lift. Mornings are a busy time, with OPDs running, and we did not want to be hopping up and down waiting for the lift to come. Moving the prime minister into the operating theatre was not only the best for her medically, it was also the safest for everyone because a sea of people could be expected to descend, very soon, on the hospital the moment the news spread, and it would be impossible for the few security guards on duty to maintain order.

Once she had been taken to the eighth-floor operating theatre, I informed my predecessor, the outgoing director, Dr H.D. Tandon, who was in the boardroom to attend the meeting being held to confirm my appointment as his successor. Since the ink was not even dry on my appointment letter, the health minister, B. Shankranand, who had also arrived in the casualty department, asked us both to take charge of the emergency, along with Dr Safaya.

There was a lot to do. A huge crowd might storm the gates of AIIMS to catch a glimpse of Mrs Gandhi or to barge into the premises to kill the first Sikh they saw. Rioting outside the hospital had already started – revenge for Mrs Gandhi's assassination by her two Sikh bodyguards, the news of which had already started trickling out. They had pumped her body with bullets as she crossed the lawn of her residence in revenge for Operation Bluestar – when the army had stormed the Golden Temple, a Sikh holy shrine in Amritsar, in the first week of June, killing over 400 people. A bloodbath against Sikhs could not be ruled out. Sadly, it did come to pass in the days that followed. Apart from preventing the violence from spilling over into AIIMS, some order had to be maintained to manage the comings and goings of the entire political class and members of Mrs Gandhi's Congress Party.

We cancelled all elective surgeries. Staff cleared the pre-operative ward on the seventh floor to make space for the deluge of mourners who were expected. All patients on the seventh and eighth floors were moved to other wards. Dr Safaya busied himself collecting blood from all the hospitals in Delhi. Mrs Gandhi's blood group was B negative – a rare group – and we had only a few bottles of it in the fridge. It finished within minutes. The doctors then used O negative blood, which is a universal donor, and Dr Safaya desperately called around all the hospitals asking for O negative blood.

Blood was being pumped into her, but it was a losing battle. She was losing copious amounts of it. Of some 33 bullets that had been fired at her, some had passed through her body while others remained lodged inside. The bullets had shattered her right lung and liver, causing very heavy bleeding. As the surgeons tried to staunch the bleeding, bullets kept tumbling out and clattering to the floor. Dr Venugopal had to change his scrubs three times – they were drenched in so much blood. The perfusionist (the person who operates a heart-lung machine) kept transfusing the blood into the vein in her neck but it kept gushing out, spilling down to the shattered lung and abdomen. The perfusionist was a young Sikh. The moment he heard the doctors mention that her killers were Sikh, he fled the operating theatre to save his life. The doctors had to bring someone else in.

We were told that we had to put off announcing her death until her son, Rajiv Gandhi, President Giani Zail Singh and others, such as P.C. Alexander, her principal secretary who was in Bombay, could arrive in Delhi. Rajiv Gandhi was in West Bengal on an election tour and arrived before Giani Zail Singh, who was on a state visit to North Yemen. There was to be no power vacuum. Rajiv Gandhi had to be sworn in the moment he returned. Until then, our job, for the next four hours, was to keep up the charade that we were trying to save her life, when in fact she was dead when she was brought to AIIMS.

Sonia Gandhi and her children, Rahul, 14, and Priyanka, 12, arrived and were seated in the anteroom of the operating theatre. She was in shock. The children looked bewildered and frightened. Sonia started to have an asthma attack. I happened to know her personal physician, Dr K.P. Mathur, and called him to ask what medication he normally gave Sonia. We administered it and she recovered. As she sat inside, the corridor outside was swarming with politicians and their wives wanting to meet her and offer their condolences. As a new person arrived outside, I would ask her 'yes or no', meaning should I let them in or not. Often, I had no idea who they were. She shook her head or nodded.

Rahul and Priyanka were later sent to the home of the Gandhis' family friend, Teji Bachchan, to be looked after while Sonia remained in my charge. She related how R.K. Dhawan, Mrs Gandhi's personal secretary, was the only person with Mrs Gandhi, along with Constable Narayan Singh and her personal security officer, Rameshwar Dayal, when her personal bodyguards showered her with bullets. A fully equipped ambulance was stationed at the residence, but finding no driver (who had popped out for tea), Dhawan picked her up and put her in her white Ambassador car, which was driven to AIIMS, where she was handed over to the stunned staff on duty in casualty.

At around 5.20 p.m., Zail Singh reached AIIMS. He looked both shocked and fearful since her killers were Sikh. When Rajiv Gandhi arrived, he met Sonia briefly in the hospital before he was whisked away to be sworn in as India's sixth prime minister. He looked shocked but composed. Later, he told me that he had warned his mother about one of her Sikh security guards because he looked suspicious. He did not stay long with his mother's body. The entourage around him whisked him away to be sworn in.

I suggested to Sonia that she should go home to get a change of clothing for Mrs Gandhi for when she would be placed in the gun carriage to be carried from AIIMS to Teen Murti House, where the body was going to lay in state for two days. We tried to embalm her body, but all our efforts failed – the embalming chemical, when we injected it into different main arteries, kept oozing out. We had to give up and decided to focus only on keeping her face in shape, and for some reason, the arteries there retained the embalming liquid.

It was our responsibility to keep the body cool and in proper condition. Professor Gopinath provided a special cooling mattress that is used during cardiac surgery when the patient's body temperature has to be kept low. The mattress is stuffed with chipped ice, the patient's body is placed on this mattress, which keeps the patient's body cold. The nursing staff gently transferred Mrs Gandhi's corpse to this mattress.

Around 4 p.m., Gautam Kaul, ACP Police, Delhi asked me if all the medico-legal formalities had been completed. I was taken aback as I had had no time to think of the formalities.

The day's events had been overwhelming. Kaul said he needed a post-mortem report (we had kept only the operation theatre notes and report), appropriate photographs (we had none) and a ballistic report (which we also did not have). I had to contact a ballistic expert on Lodhi Road to get this report made.

By now word had spread of the prime minister's assassination. The AIIMS campus was swarming with people filling the lawns and clambering onto car roofs and tree tops. I had to call the security officer, K.C. Bhatia, to come up to the eighth floor via the dumb waiter of the hospital, which was only used for carrying goods and food, so that I could give him the address of the ballistics expert to bring him from Lodhi Road to the eighth floor of AIIMS. 'Use any vehicle you can get hold of and bring him here as soon as possible'. Somehow the ballistics expert managed to push his way through the crowd outside the hospital and come up to the operating theatre via the dumb waiter to write his report after examining the X-rays. If Gautam Kaul had not advised me to organize this report, my colleagues and I would have cut a very sorry figure at the inquest that followed.

In the days after Mrs Gandhi's assassination, the shameful anti-Sikh riots broke out in the capital, and 3,000 Sikhs were butchered. Many of the injured were brought to AIIMS with burns caused by being doused with petrol and set alight. Hindu patients came with stab wounds caused by the kirpans of their Sikh attackers.

I requested the inspector general of police (IGP) to house a police contingent on the AIIMS campus to ensure that all

Sikh staff and students feel safe and to prevent any weapons from being brought inside the luggage that patients brought when they were admitted. There were two Sikh faculty members (doctors with the added responsibility of teaching) whom I invited to move in with me if they felt insecure. One of them was Arjun Singh, my chief radiographer at the time. Both my colleagues survived the bloodletting.

Many of the victims of the anti-Sikh riots had fled their homes and sought safety in school buildings. Even their neighbours had turned on them. The ministry of health held a meeting of all government hospitals to decide how to organize their treatment.

I deputed several clinical heads of department from AIIMS to run OPDs in the schools nearest to their homes. In one packed school that I visited, there was no space. I had to stand on top of a desk in the middle and assure all the victims that we would run health OPDs every morning as long as they were housed in the school. The Delhi government donated blankets, tea and milk. Toilets had to be arranged as the schools did not have enough. We ran the OPD until the families felt safe enough to return to their homes. Or maybe some never returned home.

My selection to head AIIMS had been made by the committee headed by Mrs Gandhi. She had approved it. All that remained was for the governing body of AIIMS to confirm it. The meeting where this was to happen was underway on the morning of the assassination, and it was naturally adjourned.

Moreover, a 13-day period of national mourning was to follow. The gossipmongers went into overdrive.

'You're not going to get the appointment now, with no Mrs Gandhi to push it through.'

'They won't let a woman run AIIMS if they can help it.'

'You've missed your chance. In these 13 days, those opposed to a woman running AIIMS will lobby hard to stop you.'

I continued to chair the Hospital Management Board during the period of national mourning. Once the mourning was over, Rajiv Gandhi took over as prime minister, and one of the first files he cleared was my appointment. In my time as director, I had the privilege of interacting with two prime ministers (later V.P. Singh), nine health ministers, five health secretaries and two director generals of health services before handing over the reins to my successor, Professor S.K. Kacker.

The responsibility of leading AIIMS was a heavy one. The hospital was one of the foundational pillars of the new India after Independence and was founded in a spirit of idealism and scientific endeavour. Nehru's dream was that such a centre of excellence would set the pace for medical education and research in South Asia. It was one of his famous 'temples' of modern India. Ever since we doctors had first heard about it, there had been tremendous excitement about it. I first heard about it when I was studying in England.

Over the years, AIIMS had set new standards for research and treatment, and it was my job to maintain them. I was conscious of the fact that in academic medicine, the faculty is directly involved in clinical practice, medical education and research. This synergy is unparalleled in other professions. The complex inter-dependence of these three functions is one of the hallmarks of academic medicine. Consequently, AIIMS was a complex structure to run, as mandated by Parliament, and demanded integrity, truthfulness, compassion and accountability.

I could never have anticipated such a responsibility when, all those years ago, as a little girl playing with my dolls and treating them for tonsillitis, I decided in some strange, intuitive fashion that medicine would be my destiny. It was my luck that my lifework culminated in heading India's most prestigious medical institution. In the course of my career, I came into contact with every single class of Indian, from the poorest to prime ministers and presidents. The primary physicians to these dignitaries placed their confidence in me whenever they needed help in the management of their patients, and this was a great satisfaction to me professionally and personally.

My chosen field has been radiology. Today we cannot imagine modern medicine without X-rays, magnetic resonance imaging (MRI) scans, ultrasounds, mammograms, computed tomography (CT) scans, angiography and positron emission tomography (PET) scans. Medical imaging is an essential component of the entire healthcare continuum, from wellness and screening to early diagnosis, treatment selection and follow-up.

But it was not ever thus. It took time for radiology to be accepted as a medical specialty that creates and interprets pictures of the human body's organs and body systems to diagnose sickness or injury. As I relate in this book, it was initially scorned by many otherwise excellent clinicians as mere 'photography'.

Till the discovery of X-rays in 1895, physicians had no access to pictures of what was happening inside a patient's body. Since that moment, radiologists have moved from reporting medical imaging to performing skilful procedures to aid diagnosis and treatment. They have become a core part of modern multidisciplinary team meetings, reviewing imaging and contributing to the discussion of how a patient should be treated with physicians and surgeons.

If I have been at all successful as a doctor, my success has been to pioneer the introduction of radiology into Indian medicine and to raise it to the level and role it deserves in the diagnosis and treatment of illness. My career in radiology began at the time of the X-ray machine with its dark-room processing and dripping films, and passed, in the last three decades of the twentieth century, through unprecedented changes with the advent of ultrasound, CT and MRI scanners.

The engine of modern medicine to a large extent has been technology, a story that began with radiology, an umbrella term used for a group of imaging techniques that play a pivotal role in the detection and treatment of medical conditions. Once radiology began to be accepted at AIIMS and integrated into routine clinical practice – in other words, once it had proved its usefulness in identifying abnormalities, fractures, tumours and infections – I pushed for its expansion into all subspecialties such as paediatrics, cardiology, orthopaedics, rheumatology, gastroenterology, infectious disease, obstetrics and oncology.

Today, artificial intelligence (AI) is being deployed in medical imaging, with algorithms being produced to aid radiologists in the detection and characterization of pathology. Artificial intelligence is currently being used for many applications in radiology, for example, in detecting and characterizing lung nodules, characterizing liver lesions in MRI and prioritizing follow-up evaluations, and identifying and characterizing microcalcifications in mammograms. It is a rapidly evolving technology with infinite possibilities for patient care. Artificial intelligence will be integrated into the daily work of radiologists, assisting physicians in improving their diagnosis thanks to its ability to filter through massive amounts of imaging data in seconds.

I am 95 and will not be around to see the application of AI in medical radiology in all its facets. But I confess to feeling pride in being part of this journey and to have played a part, no matter how small, in radiologists in India having a pivotal role in patient care.

In the ensuing chapters, I trace the arc of my life and career, from growing up in pre-Partition Lahore to studying in England, returning to India due to my desire to contribute to nation-building, and being one of the many people who nurtured and developed AIIMS to be such a sterling institution that it became a byword for the best patient care in the country. I joined AIIMS as an assistant professor and later became professor and chair of the department of radiology. My colleagues and I developed the department's postgraduate medical school programme, in which we set standards for radiology education throughout India.

Against opposition, I fought for AIIMS to acquire its first CT scanner and ultrasound machine. Over the 30 years I spent at AIIMS – six of them as director – I helped establish the departments of neuroradiology, cardiovascular radiology, oncoradiology, paediatric radiology and interventional radiology, as well as a separate cancer hospital.

On this journey, I met and married my husband, Dr Amar Nath Bhargava, a cardiologist, and we raised a son and daughter. The remaining 30 years of my career (from the age of 60 to 90) were spent building up Sitaram Bhartia Institute of Science and Research and Dharamshila Narayana Superspeciality Hospital, both in New Delhi.

At 90, I stopped working and began writing this small memoir, starting with my early life and the idyllic childhood created for me by my parents.

2

Family, Childhood and Partition

The moral science classes at school in Lahore were wasted on me. I used to be bored out of my mind, though I always topped the class. The teachers had no idea that the values they were teaching me were embarrassingly rudimentary compared with the exacting standards of integrity that ruled my family.

One evening, while doing my homework with a fountain pen, my nib broke. With no replacement, I was unable to finish my homework. I knew Daddy (a member of the British Civil Service) had plenty of spare nibs in his office in the house, which we rarely entered. Since he was not at home, I asked my mother if I could take a nib from his office. She told me to wait until he was home and ask for his permission. He refused.

'Everything in the office is government property so you cannot touch it.'

'But I'm going to be punished for unfinished homework.'

'I'm happy to write a letter to the teacher to explain why you haven't finished it but I am not going to let you take a spare nib.'

Even in the most difficult circumstances, my family managed to display exemplary behaviour. My grandfather's huge family could easily have become a fertile ground for strife. Jaswant Rai Taneja was a man of some distinction and social standing in Punjab before Partition. The family was considered to be one of the leading families of the state. As the son of my great-grandfather Lala Behre Lal Taneja, he had inherited all the family's land and properties in and around Multan. Apart from being wealthy and a lawyer, my grandfather worked in the judicial branch of the British Civil Service.

My grandfather Rai Bahadur Jaswant Rai Taneja, 1877–1953

My grandfather lost his first wife soon after the birth of their sixth child. On remarrying, my grandfather went on to have six more children, a total of seven girls and five boys. The girls were given as good an education as the boys, right up to graduate level. At no point in raising these 12 children did my grandfather allow any differential treatment. The words 'step-sister' or 'step-brother' were never even whispered. As the eldest of all 12, my father, born from my grandfather's first marriage, was called '*kaka*' and treated with respect. My grandfather's savings and investments were shared out equally among all his sons in his will.

Not that his second wife did not try to jostle for special treatment. She wanted her two sons to be left the equivalent of what my grandfather's three sons from his first marriage were to inherit. She was even prepared to have a third child in the hope that it would be a third son and all three would acquire half the family fortune.

For a start, my grandfather told her that they were too old to have another child. For another, there was no question of her two sons getting as much as his three sons from the earlier marriage. His wealth was to be divided equally among them all.

Raising 12 children must have been daunting but their births were all staggered. At no point were all of them living under the same roof, though my grandparents' bungalow – 4, Temple Road – in Lahore, was big enough. The eldest grew up and got married before some of the younger ones were even born. My father used to relate the story of the day his father came to him, after his wife had died, and sat him down.

'Look. You children need a mother. I need a companion. If you have no objection, I would like to remarry. If you object, I won't go ahead. You are free to say what you feel and I will abide by it.'

My father had no objection to his father remarrying but it took my grandfather some time to find a suitable woman his age, that is, in her early forties. The woman he married was never unpleasant to the earlier children. Nor was she affectionate. Indifferent, mostly.

My family's origins go back to the early 1800s in Multan in what is now Pakistan, where my great-great-grandfather, known as Deputy Mohan Lal Taneja, was a government official. Till Partition in 1947, a street in Multan was named after him because most of the houses belonged to him. It's thought that Multan, one of the oldest cities in the subcontinent, derives its name from an idol in the temple of the sun god, a shrine in antiquity. One of its claims to fame is that it was conquered by Alexander the Great and visited by the Chinese Buddhist scholar Satsang in the eighth century.

Thanks to rental income and investments, the Tanejas were wealthy and members of the Punjab elite. My grandfather was sent to Lahore for further studies. Along with Sir Sikandar Hayat Khan – a Punjab politician who served as the first premier of Punjab in the 1930s – they were the first graduates of Punjab University and, later, the first postgraduate law students.

My grandfather served as a district and sessions judge in various districts of Punjab. When he retired, he was awarded the title of Rai Bahadur, which would today be considered a Padma Bhushan, while his colleague Sikander Hayat Khan was knighted, presumably because of the Muslim bias that some of our British masters were known to have. At least that's the way my father always related the story.

My father followed in my grandfather's footsteps by choosing law. In 1925, he was sent to London and was called to the Bar the following year. He was terse when describing the English. He found them punctual and methodical. 'In India, we can turn up

My father after being called to the bar in England, 1926

My mother, 1928

at a relative's home with no notice. You can't do that in England. You have to make an appointment,' he told us.

On returning to India, my father qualified for the Punjab Civil Service and, like his father before him, served in the judiciary under the British rule. In 1926, he married my mother, Pyaar, a Sikh, when she was 16 and he was 26.

Black-and-white photographs of the time show a handsome and striking couple, tall and slim. My father stands ramrod straight in a grey three-piece suit and thick-rimmed glasses. My mother wears a Benarasi silk sari, her long, dark hair tied in a bun. She had a modern and progressive outlook that was far ahead of her times and included a fierce belief in girls' education. She knew her mind. When all her friends chatted about how the man they would marry must have horse-drawn carriages, she demurred. 'I think a Pontiac would be more fun, don't you?' My maternal grandfather gifted her a six-cylinder Pontiac as part of her trousseau.

Since my mother had not gone to college at the time of getting married, she continued her studies with my father and grandfather's encouragement. A string of male tutors came home, including an English teacher to improve her conversational skills. She completed her studies in 1930. The marriage was happy with voices hardly ever raised. The family home, when my father was posted to Lahore, was a two-bedroom flat on the first floor of a building that belonged to my grandfather, who lived nearby in his spacious bungalow on Temple Road with his large brood. A Muslim lawyer lived on the ground floor, and his two daughters, my best friends. The daily ritual was for Daddy to return home from the court at tea time, go off to the club to play tennis or bridge and return home for dinner.

I was born on 23 June 1930 at 6.15 a.m., the first child of Yudhistir Lal Taneja and Pyaar Taneja.

Like all first-time mothers, Pyaar was hyper-anxious and was so convinced that her baby girl had bow legs that she asked a doctor to fix splints. That is, until my doughty grandmother arrived in the evening of the same day, pronounced my legs to be normal and had the splints removed at once.

While playing with dolls, my mother noticed that I was always playing doctor to them. They would fall sick repeatedly. I would have them admitted to hospital for treatment. After my younger sister Pushp arrived, I was constantly checking her temperature and pulse, sponging her and taking iodine from my mother's medicine cupboard to apply to her neck, pronouncing it to be a case of tonsillitis. This infuriated my mother. 'Pushp keeps falling sick because you treat her like your sick dolls,' she grumbled. The tonsillitis came from the fact that most of the children in my grandparents' home were operated for tonsillitis. It seems that tonsillectomy, that is removal of the tonsils, was the medical thought process at that stage and I kept hearing that and adopted it for my dolls and sister.

At five, I was sent to the Sacred Heart Convent in Dalhousie. Since my father was posted somewhere different in Punjab every two to three years, my mother thought continuity in my education at a boarding school would be best. After five years at the convent, when my father was posted to Lahore once again, it made sense for me to return and attend the local branch of the school. Lahore was a bustling and busy city with energy and drive. Kite flying was a passion. There was no shortage of plays, films and concerts.

My family memories of the 1930s and '40s in Lahore – both when I used to come home from the convent in Dalhousie and later when I lived there – were of order, harmony and love. It was only when my father was given a flat chapati, not the preferred version that is puffed up into a ball, that the traditional male Punjabi in him broke loose. He would fling it across the dining table and wait for an acceptable one to be served.

It was fashionable to learn Urdu at school then and my mother was keen for me to learn, but my father put his foot down, saying we could employ a maulvi for Urdu but, being Hindus, I should take Hindi as my second language at the convent. We had a cook from Kangra and a maid from Jammu. In the evenings, we went to Lawrence Gardens (later renamed Bagh-e-Jinnah) and waited till dusk for the magic moment when the breathtaking display of fireflies would begin. Lawrence Gardens was a prime attraction for most families. Created primarily for the leisure of sahibs and memsahibs as a sort of Kew Gardens of London, the park had a dream-like beauty. During weekends, we joined the brood at my grandfather's house to play, running out into the street in the evenings to buy rasgullas from the Bengali vendor selling them from his wooden box.

The two objects I remember vividly from my home in those years are the 10 volumes of the Children's Encyclopaedia displayed in the glass bookshelf in the living room and the large carpet my mother ordered from her maternal uncle. The Encyclopaedia was not some mere trophy on display for some intellectual credentials. We read it article by article. As for the carpet, it had a distinctive pattern and had been stored in Jalandhar with other items as we left for Jhelum. A copy of this was discovered in the Victoria and Albert Museum in London at some point in time. This, at any rate, is the story that was related to my brother who inherited the carpet from the carpet seller when he sent it for dry cleaning much later. My brother, Madan, made it a point to go and see it when he visited London as it was hanging there then.

A special treat was to head off to Standard Restaurant for cake and pastries. At home, too, my mother was adept in rustling up cupcakes in 15 minutes in a very primitive tin oven, in time for when my father came home for tea after the courts had closed.

The freedom movement was raging throughout India in the 1930s, but as a member of the British Civil Service, my father kept away from it and we children were kept out of politics. We were encouraged to concentrate on our studies. My mother related Aesop's tales while combing and plaiting our hair for school. Our language was meant to be genteel. One of my uncles who used to be a regular visitor to our house was very fond of teasing me. I was telling my mother about this when he walked in and I said, 'Talk of the devil and there he is.' My father, in the next room, heard me and said, 'Little girls do not talk like this. You should say, "Talk of the angels and you will hear the flutter of their wings."'

Wanting their daughters to be 'rounded' personalities, my parents engaged a music and a dance teacher. After about a year, my mother vaguely felt that I was not progressing and sought the expert advice of one Mrs Zutshi, a music professor at Lahore University. Mrs Zutshi put me through my paces. 'This girl's ears and throat are not worth spending any time or money on,' she pronounced.

One day, an investment adviser came to visit my father at home. When he asked my father for more information about his investments, my father called me and my younger sister Pushp into the drawing room. 'These are my investments standing in front of you. I hope they will honour their education.'

'You have given your daughters Eastern values and Western education and broken society's barriers of gender bias,' the banker told him.

He had summed it up perfectly. My parents were unusually progressive in their outlook. This was the 1940s, when a girl's only future was marriage. There was no question of further studies or a career. Yet my parents encouraged all their five daughters as much as the one son, who would come later, to study, become successful professionals and financially independent.

All of us held my father in great awe for his towering personality, though, unlike my sisters, I was not shy with him. Whenever I needed help with homework or with reading articles from the Children's Encyclopaedia, I ran to him and he would sit me down to explain. Perhaps his readiness to give time arose from him being the eldest of his 11 siblings. Throughout his life, I saw people come to him for advice and he always responded generously.

'How do you manage to love so many people?' I asked him once, thinking that with every new child, his love must have been divided. 'When a new baby comes into the world, the Almighty also gives more largeness to the heart so that more love flows out of it,' he explained.

At the convent in Lahore, I hated some of the nuns. They were all Irish, Belgian or English. For some reason, they just decided to hate some of the girls. The scolding was constant. 'Why is your pinafore torn?' 'Why aren't your shoes shining?' It's as though they were itching for a fight, as though their words concealed a desire for violence. They were dying to slap us but dared not. We were all scared of the mean ones and bitched about them. 'Let her go to hell,' I'd say about a particularly malevolent one. Not the kind of language my father ever heard me use, thankfully, but it was required on these occasions!

Convent life taught me discipline, something that has stayed with me throughout my career. When I was at AIIMS, some people were scared of me because of my insistence on discipline. 'If Dr Bhargava is on leave, just install a scarecrow of her somewhere,' they used to say. 'It's enough to make everyone behave.'

As I said earlier, when my father was posted to Lahore in 1940, I was transferred to the Lahore branch of the Sacred Heart Convent after five years at the boarding convent in Dalhousie. After passing Class 10 in 1945, I started college in Jullundur at 15 years of age. Given that the family had only 'black coats' and no 'white coats', it's a mystery why I chose the science stream and later medicine. According to my mother, it came from a strong desire to treat the sick. If anyone fell or injured themselves at the convent, I was always the first to tie a bandage or take them to the sick room, but I really don't know how justified this theory of hers is and I wish I had a better understanding of the impulses that prompted me to take up medicine.

The only time I quarrelled with my father was when an uncle of his sent his guru to stay with us. None of us believed in gurus but my father agreed to put him up for his uncle's sake because this was just after Partition and his uncle had been uprooted from Multan and my father did not want to add to his suffering by refusing to accommodate his guru. The guru, who was blind, greeted me by placing his hands on my head in the usual gesture of a blessing but his hands did not stop there. To my acute embarrassment, they slithered down my entire torso while he felt every curve and undulation. Livid, I told my mother about it but, typical of those times when such things were swept under the carpet, she did not mention it to my father, though she was, of course, annoyed. I argued vehemently with my father about this so-called 'guru' and what a fraud he was but without telling him what had happened. Many years later, when my parents had retired and lived in Nizamuddin West, my father called me over one day to see the 'guru' who was in town. Everyone in the family obeyed my father's summons to meet him. I refused.

Partition shattered our gentle world, uprooted everyone and sent us packing to India – alive but empty-handed. With Partition, we fled, leaving behind all the family properties in Lahore and Multan.

In 1947, as Partition loomed, my mother was dead set against leaving the family home and pulling the children out of school. But the decision was made for the family when riots broke out in Rawalpindi and later spread like wildfire throughout Punjab. Before the violence broke out, my grandfather had taken some of his children to spend the summer holidays in Manali. They heard of the riots, of course, but assumed the violence would subside and they would be able to come home. They never returned to Lahore. They were forced to travel from Manali to Amritsar once the Radcliffe Line was announced.

My father had been posted to the city of Jhelum, now in Pakistan, in April 1947, a few months before the Radcliffe Line was declared as the boundary between India and Pakistan on 17 August 1947. In early August, he was ordered to go to Amritsar to replace the judge there. Then he heard that the judge had been killed in a bomb blast.

Since the trains were still running amid the chaos, the Amritsar High Court contacted my father the only way it could: by giving a letter addressed to him to the engine driver of the train coming to Jhelum. They wrote a note urging my father not to go to Amritsar but to proceed to Ferozepur instead. When the driver turned up at the house and handed me the note, my parents were at the club. I asked him to deliver the note to them. My parents rushed home. 'We have to catch the first train out of here,' my father said.

'Surely it will be safer to wait till our neighbours are also ready to leave with us? We will have company and moral support,' said my mother.

'No. We leave tomorrow,' said my father emphatically and we left.

On the day we left, on 13 or 14 August, it was my parents, myself, my sister Veena and my brother Madan in the house at Jhelum. My other sisters, Pushp and Vijay, were in Sacred Heart Convent, Amritsar. What I did not know at the time was that my mother was four months pregnant with my youngest sister who would be born on 3 January 1948.

We had minimal luggage with us as we boarded the train from Jhelum to go to Ferozepur via Lahore. Every compartment was packed. It was a journey full of terror, though I have to confess that as a 17-year-old, I was preoccupied with my exams, which had been delayed by the political turmoil. I had finished college by then and was ready to sit the exam for Fellow of Science as it was known. Once the exam was postponed, I was anxious about when I would be able to sit for it.

As the train passed through Lahore station, I saw the platform littered with bodies – passengers on the previous train who had been pulled out and slaughtered. I will never forget that scene – it's so clear in my mind even today. Tears rolled down everyone's faces. 'Pray for the living, pray for the living, the dead have gone,' my father kept saying as people wept. My father was not particularly religious, though he always said prayers of gratitude to God for all that he had been blessed with. He taught us the Gayatri Mantra because it was a prayer of gratitude and thanks for the guidance that God provided on how never to wrong or harm someone. My mother, being a Sikh, taught us all the Japji Sahib, which conveyed the same moral.

Not only was my father pained by the carnage he saw, he was also profoundly anxious as to whether or not my grandparents and his siblings had reached Amritsar from Manali safely. (They had joined him later once he was posted to New Delhi). We heard later that the train after ours had been attacked by a mob. It was a miracle that our train went through.

On reaching Ferozepur, my father was instructed to set up a refugee camp and organize food supplies for those fleeing the newly formed Pakistan. We heard horrifying stories from the refugees who came, about women jumping into wells to avoid being raped. The cries and wails in the camp of survivors sent shivers down my spine. My younger siblings were too young to understand the tragedy but I, as the eldest, grasped the magnitude. I used to accompany my father to the refugee camps and I remember the looks of pain etched on the faces of families who had been separated from those they loved.

I heard later that my maternal uncle in Amritsar, whose carpet business employed mostly Muslims, including the coachman of his horse-drawn carriage, took it upon himself to organize their safe transport to the new border with Pakistan. He told his son, a particularly devout Hindu, to dress up as a livered coachman. They loaded as many employees as they could into the coach, covered them with carpets and drove the carriage to the border.

Other members of the extended family left their homes in a panic, the women stuffing two-thousand-rupee notes into their petticoats and bras as they left all their belongings behind in Pakistan and travelled to Amritsar, the nearest border town, to seek refuge among relatives in India.

Following the refugee work that my father had handled, his next – and last – posting was as the chief settlement commissioner in the ministry of rehabilitation, GOI. After this, he retired in 1956. He kept himself busy, though, with the odd consultation and by running the family charitable trust passed on to him by his father to help finance the education of needy children in Multan.

As a refugee, he was granted a plot of land in Nizamuddin West, where he built a house and spent his last years. His experience of Partition left him not so much with hatred for Muslims but a certain dislike and suspicion. 'You can't trust them,' I would often hear my parents say.

One long-lasting legacy of the British was his breakfast. He never had Indian food for breakfast. It had to be bacon, sausages, eggs and toast. He played bridge regularly with friends at home, aged gracefully and passed away peacefully in 1974. He was sitting in the sun at home, reading the newspaper when the phone rang. My sister passed the receiver to him. He took it and died, still holding the receiver, presumably of a cardiac arrest. He was 73 and much loved by all of us.

My mother's health remained good until osteoarthritis hit her badly and grew worse by the year. When she turned 90, we celebrated it surrounded by her children, grandchildren and great-grandchildren. She lived 13 days short of her ninety-fifth birthday. After repeated transient ischaemic attacks (ministrokes), we said our goodbyes. We thanked God for the life he gave her as our guide and love as head of the family. It was to me that she passed on this responsibility, and I am doing my best to keep the family closely knit and loving.

3

Lady Hardinge Medical College

Five years after the British moved the capital from Calcutta to Delhi, Lady Hardinge Medical College was set up in 1916, Delhi's first medical college. It was conceived by the wife of the viceroy and governor general of India, Charles Hardinge, out of a keen interest in the welfare of women and their empowerment, though, sadly, she died before it opened. The new medical college was to be exclusively for women and staffed by women. Parents in Delhi who were reluctant to let their daughters join medical colleges in Calcutta, Madras, Lahore, Lucknow, Patna or Agra now had an option. During its 100 plus years, the college has expanded to include boys for postgraduate studies. Lady Hardinge Medical College was the only academic medical institute in Delhi for 40 years until 1956, when AIIMS was established by Jawaharlal Nehru's first health minister, Rajkumari Amrit Kaur, with a view to creating not merely a hospital but also a centre of excellence in medicine.

As part of his posting to New Delhi, my father had been allotted a beautiful bungalow beyond Kashmere Gate on Club Road. After finishing my Fellow of Science, I had joined Lady Hardinge Medical College and Hospital. By then I was in my third year. In my first two years, I studied anatomy and physiology. I enjoyed visiting the family on weekends after a busy week, during which I had to stay on the campus because clinical and hospital postings had started and students had to be present for evening rounds. When clinical postings start, students have to attend to patients. During the day we shadowed doctors, and this included accompanying them on their evening rounds.

The English faculty had left by the time I joined, replaced by Indians. There were three dining halls: vegetarian, eggetarian and non-vegetarian. I joined the latter. My class of 50 young women came from all over India (though not the Northeast, I seem to recall) and from every religion. The all-women faculty, too, was diverse. From the South was Dr Sita Achaya, FRCS, professor of anatomy because, in those patriarchal days, she could not get a job in surgery. Also from the South was Dr Jessy Mathis, another anatomy teacher. From Punjab, there were Dr Mullick and Dr B.K. Anand in physiology. The college rules stipulated that the principal had to be a woman, but since none were available, Dr Amir Chand, a senior and respected teacher from Lahore, was appointed after the rule had been tweaked. Later, in 1951, a female American principal, Dr Carroll L. Birch, who had served in Africa, was appointed.

For dissection, we had to work as a group of four owing to the limited number of cadavers available. Four students had to learn from one body. In the first year, we started dissection from the limbs. Each student had one leg and one arm to dissect from the skin, layer by layer, from the muscles down to the bones. As I dissected and separated the muscles, I understood in a flash what my theory lessons had been telling me, such as how the arteries and veins travel from the centre to the tips of the fingers and toes. My dissection partner Savitri Juneja and I became good friends. The chest and abdomen were left for the second-year students to dissect so that the whole body was fully used. The lungs and heart were dissected in the chest; liver, kidneys and spleen in the abdomen. At the end of two years, a prize was awarded to the best dissected hand, of which the bones, muscles and blood vessels were cleanly dissected.

The cadavers were sourced from hospitals – the homeless found dead on the streets, accident victims whom no one had come to claim, people so poor their families did not have the resources to cremate them. In those days, hardly anyone in India donated their bodies for medical science.

I understood why human cadaveric dissection has substantial value in medical education. Not only is it vital when learning anatomy, it also helps medical students in their professional and emotional development in preparation for a career as a doctor. Dealing with a human cadaver cultivates the development of medical professionalism, empathy and respect for the human body. When you start, the emotions are overpowering. Some students feel nausea and dizziness at not just the sight but also the smell, though I did not. What I felt was that we were violating their privacy in some way. Let's face it, this is usually the first time a medical student sees a naked body, and for some, their first encounter with a dead body. Cutting, dismembering and disassembling a body is outside the realm of human experience, and it takes time to adjust.

We did not do this, but some students at some medical colleges overseas conduct memorial ceremonies of gratitude towards cadaver donors. Some have a signboard at the head of every dissection table providing a brief personal history and photograph of the donor. I often wondered why the person had decided to become a donor. Had he been a doctor? Was she passionate about scientific research. It is quite something to have these thoughts while disarticulating and bisecting a cadaver's head, opening the scalp, removing the brain and placing it in a biohazard bag. For some moments, you are very aware of them as human beings and in others, you forget their humanity completely. I felt an overwhelming sense of gratitude to the donors for helping us learn.

Physiology, the study of how the body functions, was equally interesting, but we did not have a teacher after six months, and when the new teacher came, we had to finish the two-year course in one year. My friend Kasturi Mullick and I read alternate chapters and exchanged notes so that we could finish *Samson Wright's Applied Physiology* by teaching each other and correlating it with the anatomy. I liked anatomy and Kasturi, physiology. The arrangement worked. Later, she rose to be the principal of Lady Hardinge; we were friends for life.

After two pre-clinical (theoretical) years of anatomy and dissection, our first professional examinations took place. In the third year, Dr B.B. Roy came from Calcutta to teach us drugs and pharmacology. Clinical classes included learning the art of taking down a patient's medical history and a basic clinical examination. This was followed by our second professional exams.

The fourth year started with pathology and bacteriology as one subject, taught by Dr Hira Bai Patil and Dr Son Bhatia, as our main subject, on which we would be evaluated in the third professional examination. I cleared the first, second and third professional examinations on time, coming third or fourth in the class. In the fifth year, we were in the thick of clinical work, going to the hospital every morning and evening, and taking theoretical classes in the afternoons in all the final-year subjects. We were assigned patients. It was our responsibility to examine them, write down their history, their symptoms. During their round, the doctor on duty would listen as we presented our findings. We were marked on these findings every day. To ensure we had all-round experience, we were posted in all the major departments, ranging from medicine and surgery to obstetrics, ENT and gynaecology. The doctor we worked with was the professor of the department we were posted in.

On the clinical side, Dr M. Chaudhri, FRCS, was professor of surgery; Dr S.I. Padmavati, MRCP, was professor of medicine; Dr Malkani, MRCOG, was professor of gynaecology and obstetrics. Eye and ENT were one subject covered by Dr Ruby Joseph and Dr Sheela Martin, and Dr Reid was professor of orthopaedics and constantly had her hands covered in plaster of paris in the OPD, working day and night.

We had no regular exposure to radiology apart from a few lectures. Dr Kohli, professor of radiology, used to bring a clock with her to the class. The moment she turned her back to the class to write on the board, a few girls would advance the time on the clock. In other words, no one paid much attention to the lectures. They were a lark. Radiology was not a subject on which we would be evaluated in the final examination. Nor was there, frankly, much for us to learn in those days. Dr Kohli would show us X-rays of the head, chest, abdomen and bones. 'If you have fluid in the chest, the image will show white patches whereas the lungs are black,' she would say, as an example. Without today's advanced technology, doctors then relied just on X-rays and their physical examination for the diagnosis.

The surgery we saw was mainly intestinal obstruction for tuberculosis (TB), breast lesions caused by TB and late-stage cancer, and stones in the kidneys and gall bladder. The mainstay of the hospital was gynaecology, obstetrics and advanced carcinoma cervix. For male postings, that is, to learn about male organs, we were sent to Irwin Hospital; for psychiatric postings to Agra, but this was a joke. For the MBBS exam, we needed a posting in psychiatry, and there was no such department at Lady Hardinge or anywhere else in Delhi. But going to Agra was a holiday because the mental asylum there had no psychiatrists either, even though it had mentally ill patients. All we did was observe the patients and talk to them. One thought he was Nehru. Another said he was King George V. After we were done with these mentally ill patients, and feeling sorry for them because they were beyond cure, we popped out to see the Taj Mahal and have a meal.

In medicine, we saw fever, pneumonia, asthma and pleural effusion, but Dr Padmavati's favourite was rheumatic heart disease – mitral stenosis – which we saw plenty of. We learnt the diastolic rumble (the 'whoosh' sound in your heart, which occurs when your heart relaxes between beats) that she stressed was evidence of mitral stenosis. Later, she opened the first cath lab in Delhi to confirm her clinical findings. The lab was a specialized medical room equipped with advanced imaging technology. Here, doctors performed minimally invasive procedures to diagnose and treat heart conditions using a thin tube called a catheter.

Fellow student June Pradhan and I brought home the trophy for debating one year against other colleges; in the fourth year, I was elected president of the Students' Union. It had nothing political about it. My job was to take the roll-call at 8 p.m. to ensure that all the girls were safely in house and duly report this to the hostel warden. The job also entailed meeting the principal frequently. One day, Dr Birch said she wanted to go to Chandni Chowk to take pictures of people suffering from leprosy. I was appalled, thinking that with the holidays coming, she wanted to take the pictures back to the USA. I couldn't help think that the pictures might be the medical equivalent of Katherine Mayo's infamous 1927 book, *Mother India*. It portrayed a dismal picture of Indian culture and social evils and was dismissed by Mahatma Gandhi for its distorted representation. He called it a 'report of a drain inspector sent to examine India's "drains"'.

I took a deep breath and launched into an exposition of all the lovely things in India she could photograph rather than distressing images of leprosy. Dr Birch quickly corrected me, explaining that the photos were going to be used to educate us about the disease – far more useful than teaching us about, for example, Rocky Mountain spotted fever, which did not even exist in India and which we were not likely to see. The photos were arranged for and later used in lectures that Dr Birch delivered to the whole college to stress that we must make a point of understanding leprosy and treating it. Having worked in Africa, she knew it could be prevented and controlled.

The clinical years were exciting. We were learning new things every day, albeit on a small scale, for the hospital only catered to female patients and, hence, clinical exposure was mostly restricted to gynaecology and obstetrics.

In the evenings, for relaxation, we went to Connaught Place, which had the Regal and Rivoli cinemas and, a little further down, the Odeon and Plaza. We usually went for late shows and tipped the hostel guards to escort us back to the hostel at night safely. Though there was a roll-call at 8 p.m., as long as you registered your absence, you could go out. The chana-bhatura at Kwality restaurant with a Coke was my favourite. When extra money was available, ALPS, a restaurant on Queensway (now Janpath) was very popular because it had an excellent band with Italian and Swiss musicians. There were no jaunts in the fifth year. The final exams loomed over us. I came sixth or seventh in the class. Those who came third or fourth were rewarded with house jobs, that is, real hospital work, in the college.

My years at Lady Hardinge were joyful. At no point did I feel that medicine was not my calling. From the moment I started with anatomy and studied the whole skeleton of 206 bones, which hung in the department, down to the muscles and ligaments that are attached, I was in a state of bliss. I was mesmerized at how each bone is shaped in such a way that it performs the function that enables you to stand upright, walk and protect your inner organs. The teachers in theory classes explained the exquisite details of each bone and joint and, being masters of the subject, entranced the entire class.

Before a new lecture, the teacher would check how much we had learnt from the previous one by picking on anyone at random to explain something, and so we had to be prepared. It was made clear to us that the big, fat *Gray's Anatomy* had to be learnt by heart in the first couple of years as a pre-condition of being good doctors. Published in 1858 by Drs Henry Gray and Henry Vandyke Carter, the book has remained, after more than 150 years of continuous publication, the definitive and comprehensive reference on the subject.

I found the physical examination that we learnt in the third year riveting – just the very act of putting on my white coat and the stethoscope that had been brought from England as a birthday present from my father, before placing my hand on the wrist to feel the pulse (using a watch my mother had bought me) and listening to the heart beating in the chest, hearing the sounds as the heart contracted and relaxed, and knowing that each sound had a meaning – were moments of euphoria. Every day was one of excited anticipation as to what I would learn next about the magic and mysteries of the human body. I was in the world of medicine and it was the only place I had ever wanted to be.

With my studies over, I was now an MBBS. Next was my house job or residency, a period of post-medical study that doctors have to complete before becoming full-time practitioners. As a women's hospital, Lady Hardinge had offered me limited clinical exposure. Irwin Hospital was bigger, and I tried to get a house job there after qualifying. I got lucky and was posted in the Medical Unit (or Department of Medicine) under Dr P.C. Dhanda and Dr M.L. Sharma. Dr Dhanda was the only doctor in Delhi with an ECG machine, and thus attracted many cardiac patients. As for Dr Sharma, he was called the 'Walking Price', the textbook we followed, written by someone called Price, because he knew every page of it by heart. It was hard work but I loved it and gained a lot of knowledge and skills.

My next posting was in surgery, in Dr B.B. Bhatia's unit, which was a busy unit with lots of both routine and emergency surgeries, and gave me an opportunity to assist, something I could never have done at Lady Hardinge. I was so busy day and night that my six months in medicine and six months in surgery flew by.

During the day we belonged to separate units, but for night duties, we were physicians – surgeons on call for all four medical and surgical units. On night duty, it was impossible to sleep. Every few minutes a call came through from one unit or another. The most common was having to administer an aminophylline injection for an asthmatic patient – and there were many such patients. The injection dilated the bronchi and helped them breathe. Another common procedure was emergency surgery for strangulated hernias. When an organ is displaced from its normal position and protrudes outside the body, as long as the blood supply to the organ remains, the organ can be pushed back into place. If, however, the blood supply gets compromised, the organ is termed 'strangulated' and the most common manifestation is when part of a man's intestine protrudes through a weak spot in the abdominal wall, usually in the groin area, and becomes trapped. Once trapped or 'strangulated', the intestine becomes blocked and it becomes a life-threatening situation. We used to operate to return the organ to its normal place.

The time came for me to decide on my further studies following the house job. I had to choose from general surgery, medicine, orthopaedics, gynaecology, paediatrics and eye and ENT on the clinical side. On the para-clinical side (that is, not directly involved in the care of patients), there was pathology and radiology. Or it was the basic sciences of anatomy, physiology, biochemistry and pharmacology.

I ruled out the basic sciences as they would confine me to a laboratory when my goal was to serve the ill. On the clinical side, I was good at surgery but felt unsuited for it because of the image I had in my mind – that a surgeon had perforce to be a tall and strong personality, not a petite woman like me. I had seen Dr M. Chaudhury, our professor of surgery, who was short and slender like me, and she attracted only minor surgical work. This did not appeal to me. I had something larger in mind.

Regarding medicine, my role model was Dr Padmavati, the cardiologist who set up the first catheter lab in Delhi and who taught well. But she had sharp ears that could hear all manner of sounds, gross and subtle, and differentiate between them. She could hear the diastolic rumble – she was very fond of it – which I struggled to hear. Nor had I forgotten the brisk words of Professor Zutshi, the music teacher at Lahore University who advised my parents to waste no further time on music classes for me as I had no ear for it. On the basis of these somewhat whimsical feelings, I decided that I was unlikely to become a good physician.

Eye and ENT? No thank you. These small organs failed to live up to my inspiring vision of healing the whole body from head to toe.

I rejected gynaecology and obstetrics, which most women were expected to take up. I hated the idea of delivering babies for large families, adding to the population. In those days, having six or seven children was the norm, and for me it was a simple choice: Am I going to do good by healing sick people or am I going to harm society by increasing the number of children and burdening the parents who would have to feed and educate them?

On top of this principled stand lay a second practical reason for rejecting gynaecology and obstetrics. It so happened that the first three cases allotted to me during my obstetrics and gynaecology posting were cases of bleeding during pregnancy after 24 weeks, known as antepartum haemorrhage. For this, students had to take the patient's pulse every 15 minutes and blood pressure every 30 minutes and record them, which I did, diligently. I was exhausted after doing so. When a senior student walked into the labour room and offered to stand in for me while I fetched a coffee and snatched some fresh air, I accepted. As luck would have it, the professor walked into the labour room and asked for the student on the case. The student was, of course, sipping her coffee. The professor did not know that this was my third consecutive antepartum haemorrhage case. Unfortunately for me, I returned to the labour room while she was still there and her glare told me what she thought of me for leaving the labour room. I wondered whether, even if I worked hard, she would hold this against me in the final exam. The cup of coffee proved to be my little Rubicon – a small puddle rather than a river, but just as fateful.

What did this leave me with? Pathology and radiology. Pathology was my first choice. The SWOT analysis I had done of myself had thrown up pathology as a first choice with radiology second. But what bothered me about pathology was that it had no patient contact, only slides and specimens. Radiology at least had some patient contact and possibly more interaction if you sought it. (Radiologists should not be confused with radiology technicians. The latter, while having extensive training, do not have a medical degree). Good radiologists need an extensive knowledge base in addition to skills like time management, critical thinking and complex problem-solving. They need to be able to recall an extensive amount of information, aware of all organ systems and able to recognize the pathology – the essential nature of diseases – of anything from the toe all the way to the brain.

In any case, at that time, there was no vacancy in pathology at Lady Hardinge or Irwin Hospital, but there was an opening in the blood bank at Irwin Hospital, which was attached to pathology, so I joined the blood bank while waiting out the six months till a vacancy in pathology became available. The blood bank was next to the department of radiology, and I started having coffee with the staff there. When I met the head, Dr N.G. Gadekar, I told him of my angst over which postgraduate course to follow and he encouraged me to join radiology for two reasons: the need was great and good candidates scarce.

At that time, radiology was not an undergraduate subject for the MBBS. Each expert professor, whether surgical or medical, believed they could interpret X-rays themselves after examining the patient, and indeed many could – they would consider seeking a radiologist's opinion only if their X-ray findings did not match their clinical opinion.

In short, radiologists did not command the respect that they deserved. Only those students who could not enter the fields they really wanted opted for radiology as a last resort because there were plenty of vacancies. Because of World War II, the Army needed radiologists, and many joined the Army on short- or long-term commissions and got jobs. Very few went into the private sector or academic medicine.

In the early 1950s when I was agonizing over what my postgraduate subject should be, Delhi had only three main radiology practices – Aggarwal on Curzon Road, Ved Prakash on Hanuman Road and Dr Sharma in Daryaganj, who was by far the most popular. Daryaganj was known then as the Harley Street of India, and Dr Sharma was a radiologist but called his clinic 'X-Rayist'. In the technical sense, Dr Sharma did very good X-rays, but he did not write a report on them and instead sent the images directly to the referring doctor, thus cutting down the patent's charges. I was very aware of the general shortage of radiologists from my own experience at Irwin, despite it being a large hospital, and at Lady Hardinge Medical College.

Dr Gadekar had planted a seed in my mind and it grew. Radiology would fulfil my obsession of wanting to treat the entire body, not just one or two organs. I would see the whole skeleton and the gastrointestinal tract on a film without using a surgeon's scalpel, yet help the surgeon treat all parts of the body. Further, the vacancy in pathology never materialized after six months. However, there was a vacancy in radiology with no applicants. It was mine for the taking.

Many sleepless nights followed. Should I take the radiology job for all the reasons just outlined? Or should I perhaps wait for an opening to emerge in pathology? Dr Gadekar stressed that the advantage of radiology was the shortage of trained people and that it was an untrodden path with great potential, precisely because so much remained to be explored. He said that in future, every doctor would require the help of a radiologist. Little did I know how prescient his prediction would turn out to be.

In the end, I decided to opt for radiology for six months, and when a vacancy in pathology happened, I could then make a final decision.

During this time, I interacted with all departments and patients because there was very little radiology work. Irwin had only one primitive General Electric Company (GEC) X-ray machine for fluoroscopy, which is a medical imaging technique that uses X-rays to create a real-time video of the inside of the body, and for radiology. No one seemed interested in radiology. I started reading *Radiology*, the bible on the subject, and it soon dawned on me that, precisely because it was a path less followed, it could be a fascinating career choice. Radiology is among the younger branches of medicine, but it has revolutionized the way medicine is practised. Initially, X-rays were used only to detect dense structures, such as foreign bodies and stones, and in the evaluation of bones. With improvements in X-ray equipment, soft tissues, such as breast, began to be imaged using X-rays. Thus originated mammography, which is now an indispensable tool in screening for breast cancer. At the time I was agonizing over my choice, I was not aware of this except perhaps subliminally, on the periphery of my consciousness.

My friends heard about my possible choice of radiology. After our house job, all of them had become registrars in the clinical subjects they had chosen, that is, they were fully qualified doctors who were undergoing further specialized training.

'So, you're going to look at black-and-white pictures for the rest of your life?' some asked.

My reply was, 'Who knows, they might be technicolour by then?'

These comments irked me but I somehow intuited that it was all right to go out on a limb. Other, more senior people were more visionary and, along with Dr Gadekar, encouraged me, suggesting that the amount of patient contact I would have was really up to me and what I made of the job. We all knew, after all, that doctors often 'heard' their patients without 'listening' to them. I focussed on listening carefully to patients and taking down their medical history thoroughly so that I understood, before the consultants even looked at the images, what they wanted to know. This habit stood me in good stead throughout my career.

I also understood that if I wanted a close doctor–patient connection, a career as a radiologist was not going to rule it out. After all, difficult doctor–patient conversations still had to be had. At that time, of course, I was thinking only of X-rays and what patients used to want to know. Later on, this became even truer as technology advanced further. For example, on performing an ultrasound, a patient would ask what I have identified, what I am looking for and other questions. Likewise, helping a nervous woman through a mammogram, which is a delicate moment, or performing interventional radiology, in which doctors not only interpret images but perform minimally invasive surgical procedures through small incisions in the body. One example is an angiography, an X-ray of the arteries and veins to find any blockage or narrowing of the vessels, as well as other problems. During all these procedures, patients have to be told about their illness and what the therapeutic procedures will reveal.

But if I was going to take up radiology, I needed training and there was none in Delhi. No fellowships or scholarships either. Since radiology was not covered during my undergraduate medical training, I needed postgraduate-level training. I knew of the Barnard Institute of Radiology, a centre in Madras that had been set up by a radiographer by the name of Mr Barnard, who came to India during World War II, but I judged it to not be the best place to be trained. After discussing it with my parents, who had a modern and progressive outlook, they consented to send me to England for training, even though they had four other children being educated at the time. When they agreed to make these sacrifices, I was moved and pledged to myself to make a good career out of the 'black-and-white images' my colleagues sneered at in order to vindicate my parents' faith in me.

4

Studies in Post-Empire England

I made preparations to sail for England in 1955. I was 25 years old. I had been accepted for the diploma in medical radio diagnosis (DMRD) course which was part-physics, part-clinical. The physics teaching was at Guy's Hospital and the clinical work was at Westminster Hospital. At the train station in New Delhi, my family gave me a happy floral send off as I boarded the Frontier Mail, accompanied by my father, to Bombay.

From Bombay, I sailed on MV *Asia*, a journey that would take 10 days, via the Suez Canal and the Mediterranean through to the port of Genoa in Italy, Calais in France and then the famous white cliffs of Dover. The ship was full of students, with plenty going on during the day and dancing and singing concerts in the evening, led by the ALPS band from Delhi. Apart from the initial sea sickness up to Yemen, I enjoyed every moment of the journey.

On reaching London, we were met at Victoria train station by a representative of India House, a student residence in Highgate, who had arranged for a week's accommodation at the YMCA for male students, and Dr Sneh Taneja was on that list. There was no YWCA, and the representative was

At the Paris station enroute to England. Station employees were on a strike and there was no coffee available.

confounded and did not know where to put me. Fortunately, my uncle lived in London and he took me in for the night. But since he was leaving for India the next day, I arranged to move in with my school friend Romala Bhandari, who was living temporarily at the Methodist International House in Bayswater. We went to India House for help in finding a flat, but nothing on its list was suitable and time was short before our classes began. It was early post Independence, and Indians were looked down upon as former brown subjects not fit to be accommodated. Romala and I scanned the evening papers and called landladies only to be refused the moment we revealed our nationality.

We put the word out to everyone we knew, and finally a family friend mentioned a flat at Barons Court in West London. The flat belonged to a Mr Mackenzie who had been posted in India with Unilever and was now living in Egypt. He had no bias against Indians and let us move into what turned out to be a lovely second-floor flat. He even had Bombay Dyeing bedsheets, which made us feel at home. The flat was not centrally heated and you had to insert shillings into the electricity meter for light and to turn a small heater on. A cleaning woman came once a week to clean the flat, polish the parquet flooring and scrub the oven and bathroom.

Dr Peter Kerley was the chief of radiology at Westminster and was a famous name as one of the editors of *A Text-book of X-Ray Diagnosis by British Authors*, published in three volumes in 1938. For many years, it was *the* reference book of radiology – a must for anyone interested in the subject. Dr Kerley discovered several of the medical signs used in interpreting radiographs. He became famous for his 'B' lines. Kerley B lines are a finding of congestive heart failure. These are short, parallel lines perpendicular to the lateral lung surface, indicative of increased opacity in the pulmonary septa. I looked upon Dr Kerley, a stern Irishman who had won many honours and awards during his career, with admiration and awe, not just because of his groundbreaking findings but also because, when I looked at the same X-ray, I could not even see the pulmonary arteries, leave alone the pulmonary veins or lymphatics or the famous B lines.

All I had learnt so far in India about looking at X-rays was 'heart is normal, lungs are clear', even though it had been about half a century since German physicist Wilhelm Conrad Röntgen had discovered their potential to provide a non-invasive method to investigate inside the body. Given the rank novice that I was, the course began with me being posted outside the dark room to check the quality of the X-rays. First was checking that the patient had been positioned properly so that the rays let loose by the X-ray tube were directed to the precise part of the body that needed investigation. Positioning is very important if the clinician is to see the relevant part to confirm his or her diagnosis. For example, in a chest X-ray, the patient is asked to take a deep breath so that the diaphragm is pushed down to the level of the last ribs, allowing the lungs to be fully seen. Without this correct positioning, we could miss an abnormality of the lungs. This applies to the entire body.

Once positioned properly, the image is recorded on film. Then the film has to be processed, which was quite a laborious task – it was developed in a solution in a large container before being placed in another container to fix the image. In the third phase, the image has to be washed clean of the developing and processing solutions under running water for one hour. Unless the solutions have been removed thoroughly, the image cannot be seen clearly. It is imperative to ensure that every film that comes out of the dark room is washed meticulously before it goes into the dryer.

As to exposure, measured in milliamperes and kilowatts or 'MaKv', each machine has a chart depicting what the required exposure is for various parts of the body so that the radiographer sets it right, after allowing for some variation depending on the patient being thin or fat. The darkroom assistant is responsible for processing the films by fixing them in a hanger, dipping the film in a processing solution for a fixed period of time, putting it in a washing tank to stop the processing and clearing the processing solutions when the film is fully developed so that the film can be checked against a light fixed in the dark room. Then the film is put under running water for one hour before being put in the dryer. Finally, it is ready for viewing by the radiologist.

Remember, all these steps were manual. Mistakes could happen at any stage and produce images that suggested disease when in fact all that happened is that the procedure had not been properly followed. My job was to check that the positioning of the patient, exposure and processing were carried out correctly. This exercise taught me the importance of quality at a granular level so that I could gain the confidence of the clinicians. The chief of orthopaedics, Sir Stanford Cade, required films with soft-tissue exposure and also with osseous exposure in all bone tumours, and you could not afford to skip that protocol, otherwise all hell would break loose. Bones need high exposure. Tissue, muscle and skin require low exposure. Sir Cade wanted two separate X-rays. For example, in an X-ray where a bone tumour was suspected, Sir Cade would want to know the extent and type of tumour because his treatment would depend on it – would it be just surgery or radiotherapy or both? Since bones and the sub-tissues surrounding the bone required different exposure, the process was very precise. Malignant bone tumours, when they progress, break through the bone and enter the soft tissues, showing they are advanced tumours. Benign tumours confine themselves, with sharp outlines, to inside the bone, and soft tissue is not affected. Tumours that contain cartilage are usually better seen in the bone exposure and these are usually benign. This cuts down the differential diagnosis for the surgery.

I was the only female student in Westminster Hospital's radiology department. I felt a little odd the first few days, but as I am not shy and there were so many students from other countries, we were curious about one another and soon became friends, often heading out for lunch together at a nearby restaurant. As the only woman, Dr Kerley suggested that I could hang my coat in the radiographers' room, as most of the employees were female. But the chief radiographer seemed to be unaware that the sun had set on the British Raj and she oozed superiority. She resented my intrusion into her space. I turned a blind eye to her behaviour. She only softened much later when she saw me on television. I appeared in a BBC programme featuring Indian students in England who were meeting the famous actor Roger Moore (who later played James Bond). I was also invited to the Chelsea Flower Show, where Princess Elizabeth and Princess Margaret were the chief guests and the Indian High Commissioner was also present. After these little social triumphs, she changed her attitude towards me. From a stiff 'good morning' through pursed lips, she graduated to having friendly chats with me. She even complimented me on my saris, which I made a point of wearing in order to hold on to my Indian identity.

There were other random incidents of racism and they disgusted me. But I ignored the racism because none of it interfered with my life as a student or radiologist. Nor did it affect my social life. Some consultants and registrars were aloof, others were friendly. One of the consultants, Dr Peter Swann, invited me to spend a weekend at his farmhouse a few kilometres away. He had five children – a rarity in those days in England – and I had lots of fun playing with them. The big noisy house made me feel at home.

Once, I invited Dr Holish, the chief registrar at Westminster Hospital, to come home for an Indian meal, which she enjoyed. She was a single, white South African who was always immaculately dressed and groomed. She introduced me to the beauty parlour she used to go to for weekly facials and for haircuts. I too went occasionally.

One of my landladies, later, was an art teacher, and she and her husband often had me over for tea. She taught me the skill of perspective, which has remained with me ever since. The tea, she explained redundantly while pouring me a cup, had come from India.

My next posting was in the reporting room with all the registrars who were all male except for Dr Holish, the head who assisted Dr Kerley at his Harley Street clinic in the evening and was known to be very efficient and knowledgeable. All we had in those days were X-rays as the sole imaging modality, along with the odd Porto venogram (a diagnostic procedure that uses X-ray images to examine the portal venous system) and the direct puncture of the aorta, which only Dr Holish was permitted to perform. Once in a while, I had the chance to assist

My physics class at Guy's Hospital Medical School. 1955–1956. I am the only lady in a sari. The other lady is the department secretary.

her. Single films were made as there were no cassette changers or injectors. Twice a week I would go to Guy's Hospital for classes in physics.

After clearing physics, I was to start clinical work at Westminster Hospital for the next 18 months. It was customary for all teaching hospitals in London to make their X-ray libraries open to students in the evenings, and I made full use of this facility, visiting the libraries of St George's Hospital, Middlesex Hospital, the Royal Orthopaedic Hospital, Royal Brompton Hospital for chest diseases, Hammersmith Hospital for cardiology and radiology, National Hospital for Neurology and neurosurgery, Queen Square, for nervous disease, St Thomas' Hospital and Great Ormond Street Hospital for Children. The libraries had histories and even pathological diagnosis alongside the X-rays, which were very instructive. There were thousands of envelopes arrayed in these libraries containing images, details of the patient and their symptoms, when and if a biopsy was ordered to study the cells in the specimen. I looked and looked at these images to familiarize myself with how different conditions looked. My eye was trained in depth through this exercise. If your eye is not trained, you will not even see what is on the image. With training, you end up seeing what others cannot.

When not studying, I visited historical sites in and around London. Having been educated in English schools, I knew English history. My father had also taught me a lot of English history. But I noted, as I toured London, that despite the Empire, there was never any information available about Indian history. I embodied this ignorance too, not even knowing the Kohinoor diamond in the British Crown jewels had been looted from India.

Once my two years of training were over, I passed the DMRD exam. For practical experience, I opted to do a registrarship at the Watford Peace Memorial Hospital for a year. The radiology head visited twice a week, and I was the boss for the rest of the week. Mr Beedle, the chief radiographer, helped and guided me in my first barium meal study and throughout the entire year.

My training at Westminster enabled me to do good quality reporting of plain, abdominal and chest radiology (the only image format available at that point) and single-contrast barium studies of the gastrointestinal tract and IVPs or intravenous pyelograms. The first uses barium to image the gastrointestinal tract. The barium outlines the structures of the tract, making them more visible on an X-ray. The IVPs are an X-ray imaging test that uses a contrast dye to produce images of the urinary tract. It can help diagnose problems with the kidneys, bladder, ureters and prostate.

The clinical consultants were satisfied with my reports, and I earned enough to take a holiday to Europe during the summer, visiting France, Italy, Austria and Switzerland. I went on my own and enjoyed the castles, churches and museums. The highlights were the lakes in Switzerland and the delicious strawberries that were totally unlike the small, dry specimens I had bought occasionally from a street vendor in Connaught Place; a cable car ride in Austria on which, sadly, I lost the precious watch that my father had given me when I qualified for medical college; a gondola ride in Venice where I also had my first taste of prawns; the church bells ringing in Salzburg all across the town from 4 a.m. till 9 a.m. and seeing the Mona Lisa at the Louvre followed by a lowbrow tour of the nightclubs of Montmartre.

In Italy, when I saw Leonardo da Vinci's paintings and drawings, I realized with surprise that he was actually an accomplished anatomist who studied every muscle of the body in detail. I was fascinated by the intersection of science and art.

Leonardo da Vinci was one of the greatest anatomists ever to have lived. He dissected more than 30 human corpses, exploring every aspect of anatomy and physiology, and recorded his findings in drawings of unparalleled beauty and lucidity. Even his notes were written with amazing insight. If doctors had been able to benefit from his knowledge – in the sense that if he had published a book of his findings – medicine would have advanced in one big leap, but his findings remained in his personal papers. As Sir Robin Mackworth-Young, librarian of Windsor Castle, wrote of him: 'In the primitive conditions of the late fifteenth century, and with no medical training, this astonishing man acquired a knowledge of human anatomy far in advance of the medical profession of his day. And the studies in which he recorded his findings bear comparison as works of art with his exquisite portrayals of the exterior of the human form and of horses, or with his dramatic representations of mountainous landscapes.'* Seeing his marvellous drawings – there are some 50 of them – gave me a new appreciation of my undergraduate anatomy classes.

My time in England was productive and educational. Socially, too, I enjoyed my experience. At the professional

---

*Sir Robin Mackworth-Young, 'Preface', in Kenneth D. Keele and Jane Roberts, *Leonardo da Vinci: Anatomical Drawings from the Royal Library, Windsor Castle*, The Metropolitan Museum of Art, 1983.

level, the English were polite and generally aloof. I appreciated their punctuality and methodical approach but I knew they kept a distance. They had an air of superiority and did not mix freely with us Indians. I noted how proud they were of their monarchy. Even back then, every single action of any member of the royal family hit the headlines. In 1948, the embattled king of Egypt, King Farouk, said that 'soon there will be only five Kings left – the King of England, the King of Spades, the King of Clubs, the King of Hearts and the King of Diamonds.'*
He was not far off the mark.

In those days, I was so engrossed in my work that I was not very critical of the English. As the years passed, though, and I came to learn about how they had looted India and destroyed our culture – all thanks to a small trading company headquartered in a tiny lane in London – I became much more critical.

By now, I had a diploma in radio diagnosis from the Royal College of Physicians and Royal College of Surgeons, and one year's practical experience. What next? The choice was to join a diploma in medical radio therapy (DMRT) in England or return home with only diagnostic qualifications and training.

In England, radiology as a subject was initially considered as one that included radiodiagnosis and radiotherapy. As further developments took place in these subjects, England separated the courses into two. One was the DMRD, and the other was the DMRT.

In India, these courses were not separated at that time (the bifurcation came later) and radiologist diagnosis and therapy

---

* Susan Ratcliffe (ed.), *Oxford Essential Quotations (4 ed.)*, Oxford University Press, 2016.

were, for the purposes of employment, effectively one subject. I turned to Dr Gadekar for advice on whether I should return home with only a diagnostic degree or spend another 18 months in England to study radiotherapy (which I was not keen on). Dr Gadekar advised me to return home, saying the division of diagnosis and therapy would eventually take place in India too. Meanwhile, he had moved from Irwin Hospital to the newly set up AIIMS in Delhi and he urged me to return because India had so few trained radio diagnosticians. The hospital had not yet started clinical services but he thought I should join once it did.

Since I was unenthusiastic about studying radiotherapy, I took his advice and sailed for home in January 1958, without any job to go to.

5

The Start of My Career in Radiology and My Married Life

On reaching Delhi, I found that nothing had changed at Lady Hardinge Medical College since I had left in 1953 and Irwin Hospital was expanding to include a medical college in an area adjoining Tihar Jail.

I found myself in limbo. I had no desire to join Lady Hardinge because it was stagnating as an academic medical institution. But clinical services were not yet up and running at the new AIIMS. My aim was to gain more experience before joining AIIMS, and that left Irwin Hospital. There were four consultants in the department. The chief, Dr Bhardwaj, was the youngest. Dr Raina was constantly in the courts answering medico-legal queries as he neared retirement. Dr Dhar, a chain-smoker, was often at the police station defending reports and who was also nearing retirement. Dr Datta was an easy going Bengali and constant coffee drinker, who was also near retirement.

There was so much work that Dr Bhardwaj could hardly cope. The only vacancy was for a junior assistant who was not required to stay on the campus. I decided that this job at a

1,000-bed hospital that I was familiar with would provide me with plenty of experience.

Tuberculosis of the chest was rampant back then. It was routine in the course of a normal day to fluoroscope at least 100 patients to exclude pulmonary tuberculosis in the OPD, and send them to the TB hospital if positive. A fluoroscopy is a continuous X-ray image on a monitor. The red goggles that used to help the eyes adapt to fluoroscopy and the heavy lead apron for radiation protection were the trademarks of the radiologist. In addition to the fluoroscopic sessions, there were approximately 200 X-rays of bones, chest and abdomen to examine and half a dozen barium studies and IVPs. The latter entailed a constant threat of a contrast reaction that could be caused by the IVP contrast media.

In order to visualize the urological system – the kidneys, ureters and bladder – we had to introduce an intravenous substance that could produce either a mild reaction – itching or vomiting – or a severe reaction, namely, a fall in blood pressure, unconsciousness and cardiac arrest. We had to be prepared to deal with this threat to life. There was no way to predict which patient might have a severe reaction to IVPs. One case I dealt with was an ophthalmic surgeon in the hospital who was a friend and who was being investigated because of hypertension. Fortunately, the table on which the study was being performed was a tilting table. As soon as I saw him closing his eyes, I knew the blood pressure had fallen. I tilted the table head down so that maximum blood flow to the brain could be maintained, and then administered oxygen to go to the lungs. The patient recovered his blood pressure, opened his eyes and regained his normal pulse beat. I heaved a sigh of relief.

This reaction can also occur 15–20 minutes later, which is why it was routine to keep the patient in the department after the study for 30 minutes. I was happy that no CPR was required and I sent the patient home safely, but the process taught us many lessons. One was to take the patient's consent before administering any contrast media injection. Another was to perform the study on a tilting table. A third was to keep an oxygen cylinder ready, if required.

I have had only one case where, unfortunately, I could not save the patient. This was a young man who had only been administered a small amount of the contrast media when he lost consciousness and could not be revived, despite a cardiologist from the next room running in to help. The most difficult part was explaining his death to his bewildered family. Knowing that AIIMS was a research institute, they were suspicious that perhaps we had experimented on the young man. We showed them records to demonstrate that we were carrying out five or six such examinations every day and that they were not experiments. The family understood that their boy had simply been profoundly unlucky and no legal proceedings took place.

Irwin Hospital's chief of pathology was Dr D.N. Gupta. The other clinicians were colleagues of mine, some of whom I had got to know before I went to England. There were Dr I.K. Dhawan, Dr M. Mittal, Dr N.K. Goel and Dr Sandeep Mukherjee in surgery; Dr Abbot in orthopaedics; Dr M.M.S. Ahuja in medicine; Dr O.P. Ghai in paediatrics; Dr Mohini Karna in obstetrics. They became and remained good friends throughout my life, and I learnt a great deal from them while in this job.

Meanwhile, on the family front, before I left for England, my younger sister Pushp, a graduate of Miranda House, had married an IPS officer of the Assam Cadre. A local doctor told my brother-in-law that he had an enlarged heart and needed to be checked. I went to meet Dr P.C. Dhanda (with whom I had done my house job) to seek an appointment for him. Dr Dhanda was on patient rounds, and with him, besides the house staff, was a young man whom he introduced as a physician cardiologist who had just returned from Canada. Dr Dhanda suggested I seek an appointment with this young cardiologist, Dr Amar Nath Bhargava. After examining my brother-in-law, Dr Bhargava gave him the all clear, explaining that the cardiac image had been wrongly interpreted as a large heart. The ECG examination also revealed a normal heart. I was both impressed and relieved.

Gradually, I got to know AN, as he was called by everyone else at work because there were four other Bhargavas, but I preferred to address him as Amar. He had a regular job at General Hospital in Ottawa, Canada, where he had spent 11 years and had a return ticket in his pocket. He was on a home visit and had no intention of exploring his chances in India. My first impression of him was positive. I found him to be very professional, knowledgeable and polite, with the ability to put his patients at ease, calming them down before his examination. I noted and respected his exemplary bedside manner, but I had no romantic feelings for him then. In fact, I was good friends with many bachelors at the hospital, and so far, none had appealed to me romantically. When they swaggered into the X-ray department, I'd look at them and find some arrogant or boastful about their qualifications while others aloof. In any case, I was in no rush. I was 28 and people told me I was smart and pretty. I could wait.

In contrast to the other egocentric bachelors, AN's humility stood out. I liked his caring nature. Our meetings became more frequent in the pathology department, and I began to look forward to them. We started going to Connaught Place in the evenings, either to have a cup of tea followed by dinner or to the movies. If, for some reason, we were unable to meet during the day, he would call me at home. My parents became accustomed to these calls but neither asked any questions nor objected. Wisely, my mother waited for me to confide in her. When my parents realized he belonged to a different caste – he was a brahmin and we were Aroras – it did not bother them at all.

All that interested them was that he was a knowledgeable doctor working in Canada. My father made the usual discreet inquiries and learnt that Bhargava Sr was a respectable cloth merchant who lived in Chandi Chowk (where all successful people lived at that time).

AN's biological parents had four sons and two daughters, and he was adopted and raised by his paternal aunt. After graduating from Lucknow Medical College, both his biological mother and adopted mother passed away. It was his elder sister, who was very loving, who became the mother figure in his life.

AN proposed to me, and we were married in November 1959. We were mature individuals and decided to have a registered marriage, though my parents said they wanted to celebrate it the traditional way with a flower-decked home and a reception with the *barat* singing and dancing, followed by a lavish dinner, which we did, with one exception. We did not circle the fire and repeat the promises chanted by the pandit. Instead, we signed the marriage register that had been brought to the house. The doli was a traditional tearful farewell.

For our honeymoon, we went to Nainital. By the time we returned, my mother had found us a house in Nizamuddin near where my parents lived, and my sister-in-law had lovingly set up the kitchen with all the necessary gadgets and ingredients. My mother sweetly gave me her trusted cook and we embarked on our married life.

I had told AN when he proposed that I wished to remain in India, not only due to my desire to serve my country but also to be available to my parents as they aged and entered the evening of their lives and also care for my siblings. We decided to try working in India for a year. If things failed to work out, I promised him, then we could immigrate to Canada.

Both of us kept working at Irwin and exploring our opportunities. The Union Public Service Commission (UPSC) had advertised for the post of an assistant radiologist as it does for a variety of civil service jobs, and I applied, intrigued at how the interview would go. There was a board, and to my surprise I saw Major Dr Lobo from the Army. While in London, he had been on a short deputation to the city on recommendation of my friend Col. Dr Fonseca, who had returned to India. I had taken him around all the teaching libraries of the teaching hospitals. Major Lobo was the expert on the panel. He took out a few X-rays from his briefcase and asked me some simple questions, which I answered to his satisfaction.

The next day, I went to see the chief of Irwin Hospital, Admiral Taneja, who was also on the interview board, to ask how I had fared.

'You did well and have been recommended, but you need to learn how to sell yourself,' he said.

I did not understand what he meant, and to this day I have not learnt the art of selling myself. As it happened, I was offered the job but chose not to accept as I had no idea where I might be posted.

During the same period, Dr P.C. Dhanda invited my fiancé to join his flourishing practice. Keeping my wish to explore the possibility of both of us remaining in India in mind, AN accepted the offer. They both worked as visiting consultants at Irwin Hospital in the morning and practised together in the afternoon and evenings.

Sometime later, Lady Hardinge Medical College advertised for a lecturer's post in the radiology department. I had no desire to apply. I was all too aware of the inadequate equipment and status of radiology staff at the hospital. Dr Gadekar had a different opinion, advising me to apply since a lecturer's status would advance my career. Reluctantly, I went with him to meet the director general of Health Services, Mr Swaminathan, who also urged me to apply, arguing that the female students at Lady Hardinge needed to learn about radiology. He gave me an 'ad hoc' letter of appointment, which I took, not even knowing what ad hoc meant.

Dr Leela Rao and I were the only two candidates to appear for the interview. The chief of radiology at Lady Hardinge asked me a radiotherapy question on the treatment of carcinoma of the ethmoid sinuses. I replied that I was not competent to answer that because I held diagnostic qualifications and had come for that interview. The director general of Health Services then asked me diagnostic questions, which I answered. The next day, I was informed that Dr Leela Rao had got the job and I was going to be posted to Kalawati Saran Children's Hospital, which was attached to Lady Hardinge. Thoroughly disappointed, I went to see Mr Swaminathan to ask why I had not got the job when I had been appointed, albeit through an ad hoc letter, just weeks earlier; was better qualified; and moreover, was an alumnus of Lady Hardinge.

Through a friend's father, I also went to meet Health Minister D.P. Karmarkar and explained that I had been given an 'ad hoc' appointment and now it had been undone. The following week, the earlier status quo was restored, and I was able to join Lady Hardinge as a lecturer.

The radiology department included radiotherapy and electrology. For radiotherapy, besides a Westinghouse treatment machine, radium needles were used for treating cancer. They were inserted into the tumour tissue for a stipulated period of time to destroy the tumour and then removed. If kept in for too long, they burn the healthy tissue. They were kept safely under lock and key in a lead-lined safe and the keys remained with the radiology chief, Dr X. The needles were, naturally, radioactive. They emitted radiation that could harm people. Both for human safety and for the environment, they were kept in a vault lined with lead. As the assistant, I had access to the keys, given by the chief, and it was my job to issue the radium needles and record the time they were issued and the time they were returned in a register that was kept in the safe. I had been doing this job ever since I joined the department and returning the safe keys to the chief after issuing or receiving the radium needles. For some unknown reason, just before summer vacation started, Dr X announced that she was going to check the radium needles before I went on vacation. On opening the safe and counting the needles, to my shock, five needles used for cancer of the cervix were missing, though the register showed them as having been issued and returned, duly signed.

Dr X handed me a note formally demanding an explanation. Greatly perturbed, I discussed this with my father and he asked a lawyer to frame the answer. An enquiry committee was set up by the principal, and I was exonerated because the keys were not always with me except during the period of issuing and receiving the needles. A few days later, Dr X strode in. It was about 9.30 a.m., which was rather early for her. She summoned a *chaprasi* to bring her two bedsheets and she proceeded to throw all the department papers, files and registers from the cupboards onto the sheets laid out on the ground and told him to take them away. We were shell shocked.

An hour later, Lady Hardinge's medical superintendent, Dr Nirmala Devi Chand, walked in. Looking at me, she said: 'Dr X has been suspended. Please take over the department.' I was still in a state of shock, but I pointed out that all the documents and records had been removed by Dr X, so what was there for me to take over? She was equally stunned, having no idea that all the records had ended up in the two bedsheets. There was no alternative but to sit down and create new folders and registers.

Later, after Dr X's suspension, I learnt from her trusted nurse that, one Sunday, Dr X had taken the lead box containing radium needles from the safe to the Delhi airport. The nurse had accompanied her.

'We went into the airport and Dr X met a lady there. I don't know who she was but the two of them went into the ladies' toilet. Dr X took the box containing the radium needles with her. They were gone for a short while. I waited. When they emerged, Dr X left with me to go back to the hospital and the woman went off,' the nurse told me later.

Those needles were the ones that were missing. The obvious explanation for this bizarre incident is that Dr X must have, in return for money under the table, agreed to insert the radium needles into the mysterious woman. Radium needles have to be kept inside the body for a certain period of time so that the required amount of radiation enters the tissue. My guess is that the woman was travelling and would have had the needles removed later by another doctor after an appropriate interval. Or else she sold the needles to this mysterious woman for an unknown price. All this is total conjecture because we do not know why the woman did not seek formal medical treatment. All any of us knew was that the needles – used to treat cancer of the cervix – went missing. The box was taken to the airport where Dr X met the lady. What happened after they met is anyone's guess.

Essentially, this was a criminal act and grossly unethical conduct. It came as a massive shock to me. Dr X's behaviour, even over small matters, had been cheap and dishonest. If she ordered a taxi to go anywhere, when she returned to the hospital, she would ask the taxi driver to wait while she went inside to get the money for the fare. She would never return. If, perchance, he found her inside the large hospital, she feigned surprise and said she had no idea what he was talking about. Everyone knew this about her and everyone had their own story to tell. Nonetheless, the radium needle story described a different level of turpitude altogether.

We learnt later that Dr X was known to be the richest doctor on the Lady Hardinge campus. She had built two bungalows, one in Golf Links and the other in Jor Bagh. The cost would have far exceeded her salary, and it was based on this information that she was suspended. All the locks in the department were changed. The diagnostic X-ray machine was intact, but some parts of the radiotherapy machine were missing. Based on information from Westinghouse, the radiotherapy technician was suspended. Again, my guess is that the technician was working in cahoots with Dr X for some unknown reason. As the new head, I had to look at the Atomic Energy Regulatory Board rules to figure out how to buy new radium needles and search for the lost ones. The Board also sent a team to scan the department's waste bins for any signals from lost needles and declared the hospital was radiation safe.

Soon after this incident, AIIMS advertised for the post of assistant professor. I was interested. At the time, I was a lecturer at Lady Hardinge on a monthly salary of ₹450. The assistant professor's post, apart from being one rung up, carried a monthly salary of ₹650. My training in England and my experience at Irwin and Lady Hardinge made me eligible. Over the years, I made it a habit never to interpret a film without knowing the patient's history and, where necessary, conducting a physical examination. Why is a physical examination so important? Well, X-rays are only black-and-white films detecting abnormalities that could be caused by a number of different diseases. The radiologist typically does not examine patients physically and has to depend on the history and physical examination done by the clinician. Take the case of the most common X-ray – the chest X-ray. The radiologist's diagnosis could be a loss of volume in certain parts of the lungs. But loss of volume could be caused by a tumour in the bronchus or a foreign body or an infection. The radiologist can only make the diagnosis of volume loss but not the cause. Without a full patient history, the radiologist is at a loss and his or her report is incomplete and of no use to the clinician. If

I had the detailed history and a physical examination, I could make a precise diagnosis that gave confidence to the clinician and help him or her decide the course of treatment.

If there is one thing a radiologist detests, it is a CT abdomen request with the word 'pain' as history. We need a detailed history, risk factors, physical examination findings and any pathology the clinician might be concerned about. Take this as a good example of a report: CT chest: 70-year-old man with previously treated TB, heavy smoker for 30 years. 1/12 haemoptysis. This history needs to be provided to rule out lung cancer by the radiologist.

An example of a poor report, the kind that clinicians detest, is one that describes basic anatomy as 'XR NAD' (X-ray. Nothing Abnormal Detected) and ends with 'Suggest clinical correlation' and really not very much else. I have seen a report that said, 'CT brain unremarkable. Normal anatomy.' Absolutely useless to the clinician and ignoring the basic axiom that 'if you don't comment on it, it means you haven't looked at it'.

One case that stands out in my memory is that of a young woman brought in at night after a fall. She had a requisition of the pelvis and a fracture with osteomalacia or soft bone disease, a condition that causes the bones to become soft or weak. In the morning, when I saw the films, the bones appeared fuzzy and rarefied. A normal bone has a certain amount of density, which means that it shows up white and sharply outlined on the X-ray. But when there is a low level of calcium in the bone, the whiteness is lost and the outline becomes hazy.

Through the hazy images, I detected cysts in the right iliac bone. When anything abnormal happens in the bone, it expands into a sharply outlined circular thing that we call a cyst. My first thought was, 'This cannot be just osteomalacia.'

However, as she was pregnant, no further X-ray could be done because the radiation could harm the foetus.

The next day, the woman aborted the foetus. This allowed me to arrange for a skeletal survey. The result confirmed my hunch, and I found many more expanding cysts in other bones. My diagnosis was hyperparathyroidism. This is a disorder that occurs when the parathyroid glands produce too much parathyroid hormone, which can lead to high levels of calcium in the blood and affect the bones. I asked for blood calcium and phosphorus studies for more supportive evidence. They came back positive.

I ran to tell the orthopaedic surgeon that her neck should be explored for the parathyroid adenoma. The parathyroid glands are four ductless glands situated behind the thyroid gland, which cannot be felt clinically but secrete a hormone called parathormone that extracts calcium from the bones, causes fractures and cysts in any of the bones and increases the calcium in the blood. This patient had all these features, but at that point in time we had no means of estimating the levels of parathormone in the blood or to do a frozen section in the operation theatre to confirm this diagnosis. A frozen section is when the patient is on the operating table and you take a small tissue sample, freeze it quickly, slice it into thin sections and examine it under a microscope during surgery to provide a preliminary diagnosis. Or, as in this case, estimate the amount of calcium in the blood to know whether calcium from the bone was entering the blood.

But this was the 1950s. Instead of today's frozen section and paratharmone estimation, we had to depend on the X-rays and blood reports, which is why Dr M. Chaudhary, the professor of surgery, was hesitant. She had perhaps not dealt with such a case, and moreover, this one was coming from her student. 'You and your newfangled ideas!' she exclaimed.

But I insisted, and ultimately Dr Chaudhary agreed to explore the young woman's neck and a time was fixed for the procedure. We stood in the operation theatre, tense and almost shivering, while Dr Chaudhary dissected the neck and pulled out a lump of tissue from the right inferior parathyroid region. She deemed it to be an adenoma, a benign tumour of the body. Having excised it, she started to close the neck incision. I leaned forward to say that all four parathyroid glands need to be explored.

'I was lucky to have found the tumour in the one I explored and have removed it,' she said tersely.

'Please, doctor, please explore the other three,' I implored.

She paid no attention to me, and there was no way I could continue arguing with her. The specimen was placed in the necessary jar and solution and I personally carried it to the department of pathology for further evaluation, telling the professor of pathology, Dr Dwarka N. Gupta, who was a friend, 'Dwarka, my reputation is at stake.'

It took him three days – days of intense anxiety for me – to process the specimen. Imagine my disbelief when he reported that mass was only fibro fatty tissue – no parathyroid tissue, let alone an adenoma. After the initial shock, I understood that he had come to this conclusion because incomplete surgery had been carried out, that is, of the four parathyroids, she had explored only one despite my pleading with her to explore the other three too. A few days later, the patient developed a kidney stone, providing further confirmation of the existence of parathyroid adenomas.

During the summer vacation, when Dr Chaudhary was on leave, we managed to transfer the patient to AIIMS for the management and re-exploration of her neck. To my profound relief and satisfaction, both the parathyroid adenoma in the neck and the renal stones were removed and the patient recovered uneventfully. My confidence in my diagnostic powers soared, particularly as I had never seen a parathyroid adenoma before.

6

Fighting for Respect for Radiology at AIIMS

'I have seen my death!'
— ANNA BERTHA LUDWIG, wife of Wilhelm Röntgen,
the inventor of the X-ray, on seeing an X-ray of her hand

As I said earlier, AIIMS had advertised for the post of assistant professor, and I had been accepted. To understand the job that lay ahead of me when I joined the radiology department at AIIMS in 1961, it is necessary to understand the pitiful status of radiology at that time and the primitive state of the medical technology.

I loved the X-ray. I was endlessly fascinated by the milky white and luminous images of the body against the inky black but strangely translucent background. To be able to see through the human body without cutting into it was a milestone in the history of medicine. Its impact on medical treatment cannot be overstated, and I have never bored of looking at X-rays to see the mysterious interior landscape of the human body.

Even after all the years, the moment when the doctor holds up the X-ray is a moment fraught with meaning, the carrier of good news or tragedy. The X-ray has featured in the first seconds of the famous 1952 film *Ikiru* (To Live) by Japanese director Akira Kurosawa. The opening shot is an X-ray of a bureaucrat who has worked for 30 years at Tokyo City Hall and never accomplished anything. 'He has terminal stomach cancer, but doesn't yet know it,' says the doctor, looking at the X-ray. The diagnosis compels the civil servant to find some meaning in the six months that remain of his life, a meaning that has so far eluded him.

There was also a 1963 'crazy scientist' film called *X: The Man with the X-Ray Eyes* starring Ray Milland, in which an ambitious scientist invents an eye drop formula that grants him X-ray vision, but his new powers have disastrous consequences. His ability to look through things becomes so powerful that he starts to dwell on what lies beyond our universe, to the great darknesses and beyond that darkness to the one thing even more terrifying – a great, inescapable light that could be the gaze of God or something else.

AIIMS, when I joined, 1961

Today, doctors order X-rays to diagnose all sorts of problems: a broken bone, pneumonia, heart failure and much, much more. We barely think about it – it's so ubiquitous and routine – but we must pay tribute to the X-ray because, not so long ago, a broken bone, a tumour or a swallowed object could not be found without cutting a person open.

Like most of the world's greatest inventions that were based on discoveries made by accident, the X-ray too was discovered accidentally. In 1895, Wilhelm Röntgen, a professor of physics in Würzburg, was working on experimenting with cathode ray tubes to learn if cathode rays could travel through a vacuum tube that he noticed that a plate coated with platinocyanide lying at a distance caused a fluorescent effect. He concluded that when electrons of the cathode stream strike matter such as the glass wall of the tube at the point of impact, a new radiation is produced. He named these rays X-rays, with X standing for unknown.

He created the very first X-ray scan by capturing the image of the bones of his wife's hand. When she looked at the image, his wife exclaimed, 'I have seen my death!'

For his discovery of X-rays, Röntgen won the very first Nobel Prize in physics in 1901. But he couldn't have known that his discovery would become one of the cornerstones of modern medicine.

A year later, in the USA, Dr Edwin Frost and his brother Dr Gilman Frost were the first to take a diagnostic X-ray. They X-rayed a boy named Eddie McCarthy to diagnose a broken wrist. The same year, Emil Grubbe in Chicago used radiation to treat a woman with breast cancer. (Grubbe would go on to die in 1960 from cancer due to radiation exposure.)

The news of this discovery created a sensation. It became the latest fad. Anyone could create an apparatus with a cathode ray tube and other necessary equipment and take photos with it. And many people did. Photographers in the USA set up their wares on the street to take X-rays of passersby. Shoe shops used an X-ray machine to aid in the fitting of shoes.

Across Britain, people were fascinated by the new ability to look at their own hands, stripped of flesh, with rings clearly visible around skeletal fingers. For some Victorians, the X-ray was indecent. One writer wrote in London's *Pall Mall Gazette* that 'you can see other people's bones with the naked eye and also see through eight inches of solid wood. On the revolting indecency of this, there is no need to dwell.'*

Another writer, this time in the *Quarterly Review*, was clearly sick of the craze, and wrote that X-ray demonstrations 'are repeated in every lecture-room; they are caricatured in comic prints; hits are manufactured out of them at the theatre; nay, they are personally interesting every one afflicted with a gouty finger.'**

The X-ray craze died as quickly as it was born. Within a few years, X-rays were mostly confined to medical settings.

At AIIMS, radiography was seen as so lowly that we radiologists were treated as 'photographers' or 'back office' workers. On joining the department, I was dismayed to find one 500mA X-ray machine for general radiology and fluoroscopy for barium study, and one Odelca camera for miniature chest X-rays. The latter was a screening machine for field purposes and hardly of any use in the hospital setup. Radiology is

---

*Livia Gershon, 'The X-Ray Craze of 1896', *JSTOR Daily*, 14 November 2019, https://daily.jstor.org/the-x-ray-craze-of-1896/.

** Livia Gershon, 'The X-Ray Craze of 1896', *JSTOR Daily*, 14 November 2019, https://daily.jstor.org/the-x-ray-craze-of-1896/.

Queen Elizabeth II opening the college buildings at AIIMS, 1961

technology-heavy. Every new advancement in technology has furthered the treatment of sickness. In 1961, when I entered AIIMS, we were a long way behind the rest of the world.

There were a couple of technicians and an untrained chaprasi for processing films. We had no typist. We had to write the reports in longhand on the sketchy history-requisition slips provided. We reported and dispatched the reports on the same day before closing the department for the day. The night roster for doctors and technicians was prepared by me as we could be available whenever required because we all lived on the AIIMS campus.

So, imagine that, in 1959 when AIIMS started clinical services, we had primitive radiology equipment and one ECG machine for cardiac care diagnosis. That was the extent of our medical technology. But no one felt that anything was lacking – doctors were judged by their good clinical diagnostic skills and technology came afterwards merely to confirm their diagnosis retrospectively.

Few of us knew what was available abroad and our goals were modest. When Professor Wig, who was head of medicine (and famous for the saying that no Punjabi died without his stethoscope on his chest thanks to his flourishing practice in Amritsar), was asked for his budget allocation for general medicine, he asked only for an instrument to produce a pneumothorax to collapse the lungs in cases of pulmonary tuberculosis. Cost: a few hundred rupees. The rest of the department of medicine's equipment budget all went to cardiology. Mind you, not that cardiology had anything very fancy. At the time, it had only a single ECG machine. From the budget, they were able to buy new equipment to catheterise and measure the pressure in the pulmonary artery and the heart. The ECG gives only an electrical recording of the pumping of the heart but catheterization tells you the pressure.

My years as assistant professor in the radiology department were years of fighting for more money to buy modern equipment. But first I had to change the perception of radiology as a lowly and optional extra. Gradually, all the vacancies in all the various specialties came to be filled. All departments were to run OPD services in the morning. Very soon, the patient load at AIIMS started to increase. We ran special clinics in the afternoon that continued to late evening to give staff the chance to build on their expertise.

The department comprised me as the assistant professor, Dr Shyam Sharma as the registrar, M.C. Chawla as the senior radiographer and Professor Gadekar as the head of the department. Chawla kept meticulous records of consumables, receipt and issue, and made entries in registers with military precision. Consumables were X-ray films, processing chemicals, contrast media that were issued to the dark room staff, who made them available to radiographers to carry out their work. We were always alert for shortage of stock because all our items were imported and any disturbance in imports could bring the department to a halt. We always kept three months' stock to deal with any emergency.

We were always ready and eager, but the response from doctors was mixed as some of them treated us like photographers. Often, they did not supply me with the patient's history and clinical exam findings when they sent them to me. I was brazen. I'd call the concerned clinician.

'Look, I am only seeing the image using my eyes and mind. You are seeing and hearing and examining the patient using your eyes, ears and knowledge. If you don't inform me of what you have learnt and all you want me to do is confirm your diagnosis, then I'm sorry but you are helping neither yourself nor the patient nor me. Please provide us with the essential information and we will be friends and do our best and justify our presence here.'

My goal was simple: to drag radiology from the periphery of medicine to the mainstream where it would be recognized as invaluable because of the role it could play in reaching an accurate diagnosis. Before a surgeon even thinks of operating and before a physician can start prescribing medication, nothing at all can begin without a final report by a radiologist. It is we who gave the information they needed to make decisions about whether to go ahead with surgery and whether it was likely to be successful.

The first job of the radiology department was to instil confidence in our skills and the contribution we could make. We were in constant touch with the new cardiology lab, which used our services the most initially. The most common cardiac disease in the 1950s and '60s that was being diagnosed and surgically treated was rheumatic heart disease, which occurs when the heart valves are permanently damaged by rheumatic fever that can affect the heart and joints.

For this, radiology and cardiac catheterization were required. The latter is an invasive procedure, used to evaluate and treat heart conditions. It involves a long, thin, flexible tube being inserted, usually in the arm or groin, and guided to the blood vessels of the heart. Angiography is almost always done during the procedure, which involves injecting dye into the vessels so they can be visualized with imaging.

Both procedures were necessary to assess whether surgery was advisable and, after surgery, to see how the later tests results compared with the baseline investigations. Rheumatic heart disease is a bacterial infection known to 'lick the joints but bite the heart' and the valve usually bitten was the mitral valve. This caused mitral stenosis (a narrowing of the gateway between the left atrium and the left ventricle, which can cause breathlessness because the blood is not purified) and mitral regurgitation (where the valve doesn't close properly, causing blood to flow backward into the heart). Both conditions cause breathlessness, which is usually how patients presented. The treatment for this condition is surgical. The surgeon opens the stenotic valve and either repairs it or replaces it. The two preoperative essentials are measurement of the pressure in the pulmonary veins and arteries by catheterization and an X-ray of the chest to assess the cardiac size and lung changes of the pulmonary circuit.

I was constantly evaluating lung changes in the pulmonary circuit on the X-ray for the cardiology lab. One day, I decided to see if we could predict blood pressure in the lungs as seen on a plain X-ray of the chest. Don't forget, I had been trained by Dr Kerley at Westminster Hospital, and Kerley's B Lines were the buzz word. I worked out a formula after putting all changes, that is, anything abnormal, in the heart and lungs together and arrived at a figure in millimetres. I then compared this with the figure that was reached through catheterization in the lab. I labelled the changes as minor, medium or major pulmonary hypertension.

I analysed 200 plain X-rays and compared my findings with the pressures obtained in the lab. At that point, there was nothing in medical literature that compared pulmonary pressure obtained by my formula with that obtained by cardiac catheterization. The crucial finding was that if the changes were minor or moderate, then surgery was likely to have a good outcome. If, however, the changes were severe, the post-operative results would not be so good.

This data was vital for cardiologists. As it came to be relied on more and more, my reputation and that of the department rose. Doctors started having confidence in our reports and our ability to give them findings that could be of help to them in patient care, particularly when it came to diseases found in India. If the existing medical literature had nothing on analysing the pre-operative X-ray and comparing it with the cardiac catheterization, the reason was that rheumatic heart disease was not common in the West. In India, however, it was the most common surgery carried out by cardiovascular surgeons.

This study was the thesis I submitted for my MD in 1963. Robert Steiner, professor of cardiovascular radiology at the Royal Postgraduate Medical School at Hammersmith Hospital in London, saw my thesis and data based on 200 X-rays and promptly asked Dr Gadekar if he could release me from AIIMS so that I could work at Hammersmith Hospital. The offer was, of course, declined. I was happy and settled in Delhi and AIIMS, and by now had a young child, my daughter Anju (but more on my family life will follow later in this memoir).

In line with the discipline's low status, among AIIMS students, radiology was not a popular postgraduate subject. It was a second or third choice. Even if students were interested, they were put off by the fact that, since radiology was not an undergraduate subject, they had to learn physics and revise anatomy and physiology before they could understand the technology of radiation physics, the machines and radiological anatomy. As there was no department of physics, I had to teach them radiation physics, send them to the anatomy department to brush up on their knowledge, and have them get down to learning radiological anatomy before we could expose them to clinical work and handling machines for diagnosis.

Though AIIMS had been established as an autonomous institution that was not under the control of the Medical Council of India (MCI), the fact remained that to register to practise one's qualification, one had to be approved and recognized by the MCI. Now, the MCI accepted Member of the Royal College of Physicians or MRCP and Fellow of the Royal College of Surgeons or FRCS as degrees in India, even though the Royal Colleges of England that created them considered them to be diplomas. I had a two-year diploma in radiology, the DMRD. The MCI treated it as a diploma, not a degree. If I wanted to grow academically later in my career, having a degree was essential as the diploma was considered to be an inferior qualification.

Dr Gadekar was aware of this because he had a DMRE from Cambridge, which was also considered to be a diploma rather than a degree. In his infinite wisdom, he suggested that while I was teaching, reporting and working as an assistant professor, I should also join as a student for the MD course.

I was pleased when I passed the MD exam. It secured my future. I am and shall always remain grateful to my mentor Dr Gadekar for his suggestion. Without the MD, I could never have risen above the level of assistant professor.

Five years after I joined AIIMS, Dr Gadekar was about to retire and I took on more of the clinical load. Eager to expand the department, I did some quick sums. I calculated that out of 2,000 patients who came to the OPD, 200 would have an X-ray. This gave us an estimate of the recurring budget we needed for the OPD. As we grew, we would keep needing more equipment. By 1965, AIIMS had an OPD on five floors and surgical and medical wards (for admitted patients) on eight floors. By then, the radiology department had separate diagnostic and radiotherapy wings. We were still not getting many postgraduate students, just one or two here and there.

We had, however, established strict protocols on how and for how long patients were to be subjected to radiation, and on the protection of the

Me, in my 30s

radiographer. Of course, long ago, all radiology technicians had started wearing heavy lead aprons when taking X-rays. The rays could not penetrate the lead.

I often think of the early pioneers – martyrs really, who were innocent, with no idea of the possible harm of radiation – and wish tribute had been paid to them by all of us who came later and were helped by X-rays. By 1897, people who had been highly exposed to the rays soon began getting sick. By 1910, many of the photographers and radiologists who had helped popularize the technology had developed cancer, suffered amputations or died. Doctors began using lead aprons and gloves to protect themselves against the radiation. By World War I, the popular image of a radiologist included a gloved or an amputated hand.

Clarence Dally, a glassblower who worked with Thomas Edison, would X-ray his own hands to test X-ray tubes, oblivious of the dangers. Eventually, he had to have both of his arms amputated due to cancer. He died of X-ray exposure in 1904 and is thought to be the first person to die as a result of it. He was only 39 years old. From then on, Edison lost interest in the technology and stopped his research. 'Don't talk to me about X-rays,' he famously said. 'I am afraid of them.'

Here are some of the early martyrs, just a handful, who died or suffered grievous harm for a noble cause:

In 1896, Friedrich Otto Walkhoff, a German dentist, took the first dental radiograph. He took an ordinary photographic glass plate, wrapped it in a rubber dam, held it in his mouth between his teeth and tongue, and then lay on the floor for a staggering 25-minute exposure, acting as his own test subject. It's not clear what happened to Walkhoff but his experiment resulted in the loss of hair from the area exposed to the radiation, highlighting the early dangers of X-rays and the need for proper shielding.

At Vanderbilt University in August of the same year, Professor John Daniel had to treat a child who had been accidentally shot in the head. Before attempting to locate the bullet in the child, his colleague Dr Dudley lent himself to an experiment: A plate holder containing the sensitive plate was tied to one side of Dudley's head and the tube was attached to the opposite side of the head. The tube was placed 0.5 inches away from Dudley's hair and activated for one hour. Yes, one hour. After 21 days, all the hair fell out from the area of the head under discharge.

At Columbia College a few months later, Dr H.D. Hawks, a graduate, gave a demonstration with a powerful X-ray unit in the vicinity of New York. After four days, he could see burns on his hands. The skin began to come off, fingernail growth stopped and the hair on the skin exposed to X-rays fell out.

The same year, one William Levy, who had been shot in the head by an escaping bank robber 10 years previously and who had been left with a bullet above his left ear, wanted to try out the new technology to locate the bullet and remove it. Doctors at the University of Minnesota warned him against but Levy was undeterred. Exposures were made with the tube over his forehead, in front of his open mouth and behind his right ear. Levy sat through the exposures from 8 o'clock in the morning until 10 o'clock at night. Within 24 hours, his face was disfigured, cracked and bleeding. The position of the bullet, though, was identified, which I think is a small consolation.

One of the last martyrs to the risks of X-ray radiation was Dr Emil Grubbe who died of metastatic cancer in 1960. He endured over 80 surgical operations to relieve his discomfort and to stop the progress of gangrene from his left hand to his arm. He lived in agony for many years, yet he continued to work with the X-rays. In his autobiography, he maintained, 'My courage is my work. I treat patients who suffer more or are encumbered more than me, and so I go on. By helping others, I help myself'.[*] He went on to predict, 'I will die from the effects of early uncontrolled exposures to X-rays. And like many of the early pioneers, I too, will die a victim of natural science, a martyr to the X-rays.'[**]

Meanwhile, with every passing day, others' confidence in my reports grew. It came to be said that so forensic was my examination of an X-ray that I possessed a 'third eye'. The credibility of the department grew by leaps and bounds. Slowly, word spread that radiology's reports contained valuable information for reaching a diagnosis and determining the best course of treatment. I remember one day I was away and the neurosurgery department had met, seen the X-rays and investigations of a patient and decided it was a disc prolapse – when a spinal disc's soft centre bulges out and presses on a nerve. The surgery was completed. I came back from leave the next day and the surgeon came to me with the X-ray to check that the diagnosis had been correct. It took me 30 seconds. 'No, it's not a disc prolapse. It's TB of the spine (a bacterial

---

[*] P.C. Hodges, *The Life and Times of Emil H. Grubbe*, University of Chicago Press, 1964.

[**] P.C. Hodges, *The Life and Times of Emil H. Grubbe*, University of Chicago Press, 1964.

infection), left transverse process of L2 with an abscess.' He then revealed to me that I was right because that was what they found during surgery.

Gradually more specialties, not just cardiology, started to send their patients to us for X-rays. This, mind you, was when we had the most basic equipment that was far behind the rest of the world. But when we looked at the X-rays, we were supremely vigilant and thorough and missed nothing. Time and again, I kept telling clinicians, 'Tell me your patient's history, let me see the X-ray and I will guide you to the diagnosis'.

Another example illustrates the scope of our contribution. A resident sent a patient for an X-ray of the chest who had severe weakness and anaemia. On the routine chest X-ray, I detected that the heart shadow on the right side looked a little denser than what I would normally see. I ordered more X-rays from different angles to understand what the increased density could mean. The side view, called a lateral view, of the chest showed a mass in front of the heart, which I reported as a thymoma.

At surgery it was confirmed and at pathology it turned out to be a thymoma, a tumour that originates from the thymus gland. It is most commonly found in the anterior mediastinum that is the part of the chest located in front of the heart and between the sternum and pericardium. A less thorough radiologist would have missed the density. It is known that 50 per cent of patients with thymoma suffer from myasthenia gravis, a condition that causes weakness in the muscles and great fatigue. The patient was so weak that she could not even keep her eyes open – her eyelids kept drooping. She was tested for myasthenia gravis. For the test, edrophonium chloride, a short-acting drug, is injected into a patient's vein. If the patient's muscle strength improves temporarily after the injection, it could indicate myasthenia gravis. This patient's response was to open her eyes wide for the first time, confirming she had myasthenia gravis. The pathologist confirmed the existence of the benign thymoma tumour. It was removed and the patient went home happy.

The other departments began sending more and more patients to us as they realized the value of our work in diagnosing disease – urology, gynaecology, endocrinology, neurology and neurosurgery. We were becoming a major contributor to patient care.

One day, the Rockefeller Foundation, in its wisdom, donated some equipment but without consulting us first. We were given an image intensifier and angiography cassette changer. The image intensifier had a cine camera attached but no equipment for recording, processing or viewing the film, so only cardiology could view the images.

The cardiologists could see the images on the screen along with whoever was operating the machine in real time, and they only wanted to see the heart. We radiologists could also see the images in real time, but there was no record of them so we could not report on the images.

Any other department in the West would have thrown this equipment away. If the Foundation had consulted us, we could have told them the size of the X-ray cassettes we needed. X-cassettes are containers in which you put the film. Cassettes and films came in various sizes. The standard film was 15 x 12 inches but the cassettes they sent us were 14 x 14 inches, so our films did not fit into them. We would have had to import 14 x 14 inch films to use the machine; the cost would have been prohibitive and it made no sense to incur this cost for just one machine.

But beggars can't be choosers. I decided that whatever it was, we would use it to train my staff through jugaad, and we managed to develop spleen portovenograms and aortic angiograms by hand injections. By this, I mean that if we carried out a spleen portovenogram for examining disease of the liver, we had to inject the contrast material into the spleen with pressure. Likewise, if we wanted to examine the aorta, we needed to inject the contrast medium with a pressure injector to see clearly. This pressure could not be exerted by using our hands. Since we had no pressure injector, we all became accustomed to using our hands and our strength to push the contrast medium through the syringe. The resulting image was not as sharp as it should have been but there was no alternative.

For neurology and neurosurgery, we later acquired a Lysholm skull table, a specialized medical device, specifically an X-ray table designed for taking precise skull radiographs. The table was invented by Swedish radiologist Erik Lysholm. It allows the X-ray tube to rotate around the patient's head, enabling multiple angled views of the skull without needing to reposition the patient. We were able to do carotid angiograms to examine the carotid arteries in the neck to assess blood flow, blockages and aneurysms by a direct puncture of the carotid artery. This enabled us to record arterial, capillary and venous phases manually for detection and location of intracranial mass lesions.

But the fact remained that all our equipment was rudimentary and manual. Every stage of every procedure was carried out manually, making it slow and time-consuming. For progress in chest work, we acquired the skill to manually move the X-ray tube and obtain a tomogram for further evaluation of chest and mediastinal lesions. A tomogram is a two-dimensional image representing a slice or section of the body. We had no tomogram machine. It was not possible within our budget at that point in time.

By 1970, I had become a professor and head of radio diagnosis. Radiotherapy was a separate department. One of my most important decisions was to start holding a clinico-radiological meeting every morning. By clinico-radiological, I mean a meeting where clinicians who are treating patients and radiologists come together to discuss cases. The goal is to review both the clinical presentation of the patient and the imaging results as a team to reach the best diagnosis and treatment plan for the patient following a thorough discussion. No such meeting was held in any hospital at that point. In many hospitals, it is still not held, but at AIIMS it has become a tradition. Yes, clinico-pathological meetings used to be held. These were medical educational sessions where healthcare professionals presented a complex patient case, detailing the clinical presentation and investigations, and then revealing the final pathological diagnosis. But not in clinico-radiological meetings involving mere low-bred 'paparazzi' like us – and certainly not in the humble radiology department.

I cannot overstate the importance of this decision. No one had ever held such a daily meeting before between all the clinicians and radiologists. It was unheard of for clinicians to meet in the radiology office. Previously, X-ray films and other investigations would simply be sent to the respective department – cardiology or orthopaedics or whatever. The doctors would examine them, along with the report we provided, interpret them and decide on the course of treatment. They did not meet the radiologist.

My purpose in starting this daily meeting in my department was to improve the patient's chances of recovery. Radiologists are responsible for screening patients and trying to preventatively detect any diseases as early as possible for the most effective treatment. There are many types of cancers (for example lung, thyroid, breast and colon cancer) that are highly treatable if detected in the early stages of the disease. Detection is the first step in helping guide the clinician towards the appropriate treatment.

Everyone present at these meetings looked at the reports and gave their opinion on what the patient was suffering from. 'Why do you think it's X?' Why can't it be 'Y?' 'What makes you think that?' From this detailed and thorough discussion in this multi-disciplinary meeting, a better understanding would emerge, a more accurate diagnosis and, consequently, a better plan of treatment.

Once treatment starts, radiologists play a key role in tracking and evaluating a patient's condition. Scans can clearly show changes in a patient's condition over time and can also accurately and precisely measure how a disease is responding to treatment. This, in turn, helps clinicians determine if the specific course of action they have opted for is working or whether they should change their method of attack.

These meetings mainstreamed our work. The meetings were held in my teaching room and it used to be full. They would last from one to two hours. The attendance was a measure of clinicians' trust in us, and what we learnt from each other was invaluable both for faculty and residents.

I was also responsible for guiding students on their research and theses. For the general teaching at AIIMS, Tuesdays were fixed for 'Grand Rounds', when all the departments presented the clinical work and research they had conducted. I never missed a Grand Round. It was my chance to learn about what surgery and treatment had gone well and what had not and why. I also attended the weekly pathology meetings, the monthly clinical pathologic case presentation meetings and all autopsies and encouraged the faculty and residents to do the same.

Everyone in the department was trained to maintain the highest standards. Even relations with the equipment vendors had to be maintained as it was vital to keep the machines running well; most were imported and we could not afford a breakdown. I was determined to make my department grow but also understood that we were a service department. Our future depended on how our services were valued. As every clinical department at AIIMS grew, we had to grow with them, meeting all their needs and the only way to do that was for us to match them in the skills and knowledge required for patient care.

One day, a friend, Dr G.S. Sarin, head of radiology at Safdarjung Hospital, told me that two Siemens machines – special neurological machines called 'Mimers' – were lying around unused at the hospital. He had neither the staff nor the expertise to use them. These machines had been imported for an influential husband-wife team of neurosurgeons from England who were to spend some time at Safdarjung. After a while, they returned to England and Dr Sarin offered me one machine.

I grabbed the offer and was surprised at facing very little red tape at the health ministry over the transfer. The only question the AIIMS director asked me was, 'How far will it help your diagnosis?'

'Only marginally,' I replied. 'But I can standardize the service and make it safe for both patients and staff.'

Without the mimer, we had to manually rotate a patient to place him or her at the right angle for the X-ray. The mimer rotated patients to place them in precisely the required position.

Our further growth was dependent on budget allocation that was divided in two: recurring and non-recurring. All consumables, such as X-ray films, processing chemicals and contrast media, came out of the recurring budget through the office of the deputy director, administration and finance. Equipment came out of the non-recurring budget that was screened by a purchase committee led by the director of AIIMS.

One cut in the middle of the financial year of our recurring budget had me up in arms, though the incident was illuminating because it showed how highly regarded the radiology department was. I went and told the director that if my recurring budget was being cut, I can only do a limited number of cases a day depending on what consumables I had. 'I will have to stop all OPD cases and can only partially cater to indoor cases. I have no other choice.'

He agreed reluctantly to the cut in the number of cases we would be able to handle. But to my delight, when the circular went out, the clinical heads of department revolted. They had become accustomed to the role played by my department in their diagnostic work.

I think I can safely say that we were the best radiology department in the country, not just for our high standards but also for the sheer range of specialties. I kept repeatedly dinning the importance of the five Ps to my staff: Proper Planning

Prevents Poor Performance. I had created a library of teaching films, which was greatly appreciated. The teaching films were for students but we also loaned them to other specialties for their examinations. Once, Professor P.N. Chuttani, director of Postgraduate Institute of Medical Edication and Research, Chandigarh, visited the department to compliment me, particularly on the vascular (blood vessels) work we did. When he returned to Chandigarh, he summoned his radiology team. 'Why are you not doing any vascular work?' he asked. Later, the head of his department, Professor Sodhi, called me up to find out how his department could replicate our work.

This was my dream. To create a centre of excellence at AIIMS that would set benchmarks, to add more and more specialties and to spread these high standards to all the radiology departments at hospitals all over the country.

I could see AIIMS growing as the clinical departments radiated out and separated into subspecialties. Cardiology was divided into different sections, including paediatric cardiology. Endocrinology was the next to separate. Then metabolism. Pulmonary medicine separated. Nephrology came next. New departments such as gastroenterology and immunology came up.

It was now around 1972, and I had served AIIMS for 12 years with the limited equipment at my disposal. I now had a son, Sandeep, who was nine years old; Anju was 12. They had grown up on the campus. I was able to appreciate Rajkumari Amrit Kaur's vision to build residential housing at AIIMS when I became a mother. As a wife, daughter, daughter-in-law, the eldest of five siblings and a mother, it was a godsend to be able to walk home for lunch and supervise the care of my two children. Other families on the campus offered them plenty of friends. The campus was safe. Their ayah, Mrs Sukh, was excellent, and when I left them with her after lunch and returned to finish my day's work in the hospital, I knew they were in good hands. During the holidays, they occasionally visited my siblings in Calcutta, Madras or Chandigarh. My husband was as busy as I was at his Daryaganj clinic, after five years of practice with Dr Dhanda.

Being a parent is a great joy, a profound privilege and a tremendous responsibility. I was determined to be a good mother and thought I was managing to do a decent job of juggling multiple tasks until the day my daughter taught me an unforgettable lesson. I had come home for lunch and Mrs Sukh told me Anju, aged three, was not eating her food. I went to her room, hugged her and asked her what the matter was because the meal was one of her favourites.

'What is your favourite?' she asked.

'You are my favourite,' I told her, giving her another hug.

'No, I'm not. *Jaldi, jaldi aana* and *jaldi jaldi khana lagao* and *jaldi jaldi janaa*,' she said.

I was stupefied. This is how she saw me, as constantly in a hurry and not paying her enough attention. From then on, I tried to appear calm and relaxed and not rush things even though my head would be buzzing with all the things I had to cram into my busy day. I banished the word 'jaldi' from my vocabulary. Modern life has put the female biological clock in direct conflict with our careers. How to balance my passionate desire to use science to improve society while desiring to be a good mother? Every day was a constant struggle with time and how to have enough of it to deal with work, patients, colleagues, students, family, paediatricians, dentists, teachers, home decor, gardening and, from time to time, house guests. Thankfully, I

The Woman Who Ran AIIMS

had a good cook, and a new ayah Tina, a Christian woman from Goa after Mrs Sukh left. We lived on the campus, and were a close-knit family with strong support systems. My mother lived nearby in Nizamuddin, but luckily, I was able to manage pretty well and did not have to resort to asking for her help too often, though of course she was always willing.

Still, as a mother I was constantly anxious that I was not spending enough time with my children and rushing around like a lunatic to squeeze in swimming classes at the National Sports Club of India and horse-riding classes at their school, Modern School, for them (and visits to the beauty parlour for a facial for myself). When I look back on that time, I do sometimes think that perhaps my children deserved the greater attention they would have got from a stay-at-home mother. I should have given them more attention. But I was so driven to work that staying at home was not a possibility for me. No working mother ever thinks that she gets the work–life balance. Occasionally, I would expect my mother to reproach me in some way, to complain perhaps that my children needed more of my time and company but that reproach never

With my children on the AIIMS lawns

came because she understood all too well that my medical career was my life.

My way of coping with the challenges was to be very organized. Every morning, my sari would be laid out on the bed for me by my maid, a pair of high-heeled shoes or sandals (my short stature meant I was addicted to heels) and some jewellery, from which I would choose what to wear. I never counted but I am guessing I must have had over 100 silk and cotton saris. (Age has reduced me to wearing a kaftan around the house and I no longer wear saris, but I am in the process of distributing them to former students who come to see me and ask fondly about my collection).

I planned meals a week ahead. I have to admit that from week to week, the dishes didn't change much. In fact, it was so well known among my friends that Tuesdays were *khatta channa* day (my husband's favourite) that if they turned up in the mood for it on a Tuesday and the cook had decided to make something else, I had long faces to console.

One day, when Anju was only nine months old, Mrs Sukh was away on some family emergency and, therefore, I left her with my mother in Nizamuddin before going to work. I went to pick her up in the evening in my little Fiat, one of the only two cars available then, the other being the Ambassador. My mother had given her a massage and noticed that her palms and soles were yellow, though the eyes were normal and Anju was active.

'It doesn't seem to be jaundice, so I didn't call you, particularly as she's playful and active,' my mother said.

I was relieved but I still called my husband who was on the way to pick us up. He had done a posting in the paediatric ward and was quick to see what was up after examining her.

'You only learn paediatrics when you have children,' he said to me. 'You have been overindulging in feeding her carrots. She has carotenosis.'

Carotenosis is a harmless condition that causes the skin to turn orange. In Anju's case, it was only her palms and soles. In some children, the forehead, nose and upper eyelids can turn orange.

We adjusted Anju's solid intake and things reversed. On another occasion – again the result of over-anxious mothering – I overdid bananas for Sandeep, which made his stools white. That too was easily rectified.

Working women will understand when I say that I could have availed of fellowships to go abroad but declined all of them. My work here and my family responsibilities ruled out such a possibility. I was already missing some parent teacher association meetings. How could I even think of going abroad? I contented myself, long before the term was invented, with thinking globally but acting locally.

Fortunately, my marriage was happy and peaceful. Amar never once questioned my career or the time it demanded. He was a modern man in that sense, letting me be free to make my choices and not seeking to control me in any way. He gave me space to be myself. He was considerate and loving. He loved his bridge – we had a room dedicated to it in our home – and played every weekend. I could rely on him for sound advice whenever I was struggling with a problem at work. I cannot recall any major disagreements with him. Of course, he did nothing around the house and in that sense, he was a typical Indian man, but not in the more important ways. If our cook was on leave, he would make a grand gesture of coming into the kitchen and offering to 'cook' when we both knew he would mess up beating an egg. Though he had lived alone in Ottawa for 11 years, he had been spoiled by the nursing staff who fed him pork chops washed down with beer. To be fair, I also was no cook but having watched my mother prepare meals, I at least had a theoretical understanding of what it took and could apply that understanding to reality to some extent.

Meanwhile, he was very busy with his own practice and also working as a consultant at Irwin Hospital. However, Sir Ganga Ram Hospital, which had been established in Lahore as a trust hospital, was trying to establish a branch in Delhi but was having constant labour and teething problems. A few consultants from Irwin Hospital saw this as an opportunity and approached the trustees of Sir Ganga Ram to volunteer and run the hospital. One of them was my husband. On the new board that was formed, he was appointed as chief physician and director of the laboratories.

Today, Sir Ganga Ram Hospital is one of the leading hospitals in the capital. My husband contributed to building the department of medicine, expanding the subspecialty, and served as the director of the laboratories. He remained attached to the hospital till the age of 70, subsequently becoming emeritus consultant. He worked till the last day of his life.

Coming back to my years as a young mother, with time, my children were able to look after themselves with the help of my husband and parents. They studied at Modern School and were doing fairly well. Anju had already made up her mind that medicine was not for her. She had seen far too many sick patients walking through the gates of the hospital wailing in pain or bleeding or being rolled in wheelchairs or stretchers with broken bones. Illnesses were not something she felt ready to deal with. Rather, she wanted to travel the world and learn about other countries and their people. Sandeep was a good all-rounder at school but was too young to know yet what he wanted to do later in life.

The day came for me to tell them that I thought they were old enough for me to avail myself of study leave. What was happening in radiology in the great big world beyond New Delhi? I knew technology had advanced by leaps and bounds but my knowledge was limited to reading articles. I wanted to get my hands on the latest equipment. I wanted to bring it to India.

I applied for a WHO fellowship to visit the best radiology centres in the world to update myself: Europe, England and the USA. In 1972, I got the fellowship and I started sending out letters to the heads of departments to plan my trip.

I sat the children down and explained my plans to them. I instructed them to write to me every week. It was hard to connect by telephone and mobiles were still in the future. Knowing they were in good hands with Amar and my parents, I was able to leave the country with a clear conscience. On my return, laden with cheeses and chocolates, I found them happy and contented.

7

Turning to the West for the Best Technology

I had started my WHO fellowship to travel abroad to learn new technology. After 12 years at AIIMS, I was on a trip to Scandinavia, England and the USA. Radiology had become hugely exciting. The CAT scanner, also known as CT scanner, and ultrasound were cutting edge machines.

Before the CT scanner, the only imaging device we had was the X-ray machine, which allowed doctors to see only the bone, not the soft tissue. Invasive techniques had to be used if we wanted to see the gastrointestinal tract or the kidneys. The CT scanner was a miracle. It allowed us to see the soft tissue and bones separately, as though the body was being sliced like a loaf of bread – you could see each part. At this stage, only the head scanner had been built but this alone was marvellous. Previously, we could see only the skull but not the brain. Now we could see the brain – some parts solid, some parts liquid – separately from the skull. Earlier, for our diagnosis of, say, a brain tumour, we had to rely solely on the symptoms reported by the patient and angiograms. With the head scanner, we could see the tumour clearly along with its size, site and even, to some extent, the cell type.

Likewise, the ultrasound. We could see the foetus for the first time, an astonishing moment. The ultrasound was non-ionizing technology, which means it emitted no radiation that could harm the foetus, the mother or any part of the body. We could monitor the health and growth of the foetus through pregnancy. Later, of course, we used the ultrasound for the entire body, to see the liver or the spleen or all the soft tissues, which could not be seen by X-rays. It led us to quicker and more accurate diagnoses and with no radiation.

With the CT scanner and ultrasound available, I wanted to move radiology from the basement of medicine to the sunlit uplands of the mainstream. Yet, the resistance I encountered at AIIMS was not only from those who funded the hospital but from some doctors themselves who seemed not to realize what a gigantic leap had been made abroad. From having to use an invasive injection, with all its attendant risks, in order to see the kidneys clearly on an X-ray, to an ultrasound that allowed us to move the patient around and see the kidneys from different angles, yielding more valuable information and being totally non-invasive and safe.

As an example of doctors' resistance to new technology – and of the wall that loomed whichever way I turned in India – one example suffices. At an annual meeting of the Association of Surgeons of India, a doctor put up a picture with black-and-white splotches on it. 'This,' he said, 'is the surface of the moon.' Then he put up another picture, also with black-and-white patches. 'This,' he said, 'Is an ultrasound of the liver. How can we trust this technique?'

This kind of attitude bewildered me. But here I was, inside Dr Holm's Herlev Hospital, where the level of automation stupefied me. At AIIMS, when we wanted to X-ray someone who had been admitted to a ward, we had to send an orderly up to the ward to move the patient from the bed onto a gurney. A nurse accompanied the orderly and pushed the patient down the corridor into the nearest lift that brought the patient down to the department where we were waiting. The nurse and orderly waited until the X-ray was done. Then the whole procedure was repeated in reverse.

At Herlev, the nurse in the ward pressed a button. The patient was moved from the bed to a gurney that rolled into the lift, unaccompanied. When the lift door opened, the technologist in the ultrasound department simply pulled the gurney into the department and carried out the procedure. No human help was required at any stage.

All specimens for the lab were delivered, untouched by hand, to the lab through a system of passage tubes with total precision, unlike in India where an orderly was told to take a specimen from radiology to the laboratory by hand. He would probably wander off for a chat, some chai, a smoke – and these days a check of WhatsApp messages – before delivering the specimen to the lab.

Today, of course, automation in top Nordic hospitals has transformed the very landscape. Mobile robots are used to handle logistical tasks. They ease staff workloads and free up time for patient care by handling all manner of administrative processes that are usually time-consuming and prone to error. Self-driving autonomous mobile robots deliver laundry and meals, transport blood samples to labs and bring medicines and medical equipment to wards. They remove rubbish. They take hospital elevators by themselves. In addition, of course, robotic-assisted surgery is well known. Its benefits are more precision, less damage and pain, faster patient recovery, better ergonomics for surgeons and significant holistic cost-savings. Artificial Intelligence will bring yet more radical changes.

Copenhagen was not my first stop – I went first to Norway, Sweden, England and the USA before visiting Denmark much later in 1980 – but I relate the story to demonstrate the gulf between AIIMS's basic equipment and what the most advanced hospitals in Scandinavia were able to deploy. I was on a mission: Identify the equipment that we could use to benefit our patients, persuade the authorities to let us buy the machines and train our staff to use them, even if it meant sending them abroad for the training.

Another moment when the gulf was brought home to me was earlier on my three-month odyssey when I was at the Massachusetts General Hospital in Boston, which is attached to Harvard University. Dr Juan Taveras was chairman of the radiology department and was considered the guru of neuroradiology, having published a textbook on it which was considered the bible. Next to radiology was an experimental lab. I asked Dr Taveras if I could learn and practise the Seldinger technique on the dogs. The technique is named after the Swedish radiologist Sven Ivar Seldinger who introduced the procedure in 1953 to obtain safe access to blood vessels and other hollow organs. It is a minimally invasive procedure that involves inserting a catheter into a blood vessel or body cavity using a guide wire.

The desired vessel or cavity is punctured with a sharp hollow needle, with ultrasound guidance if necessary. A round-tipped guidewire is then advanced through the lumen, or the hollow bore, of the needle, and the needle is withdrawn. A sheath or blunt cannula can now be passed over the guidewire into the cavity or vessel. Alternatively, drainage tubes are passed over the guidewire. After passing a sheath or tube, the guidewire is withdrawn. Even today, it is the technique of choice for many people. It is used for angiography, insertion of the leads for an artificial pacemaker or implantable cardioverter-defibrillator, and numerous other procedures.

Dr Taveras agreed, and my work in the lab allowed me to become well practised in the technique, well enough to be able to train others on my return to AIIMS. At this hospital, the rule for all guide wires and catheters for angiography – a type of X-ray to examine the health of blood vessels – was 'one-time use', after which they were discarded. Knowing such luxuries were not possible in the Indian setting where there were shortages of most things, I asked for his permission to have the guide wires and catheters sterilized so that I could pack my suitcase with them and take them home. For one thing, there was no budget for me to return to Delhi and buy this equipment. For another, no one would agree to fund any purchases until they had seen good results. This meant that I had to use them on patients, prove the usefulness of the technique and only then hope to introduce them for patient use.

One day, Dr Taveras advised me to attend an annual neuroradiology workshop in New York. I went there little expecting what was to follow. The printed programme said Dr James W.D. Bull, the English guru of neuroradiology and chief of neuroradiology Queen Square Institute of Neurology in London, would be introducing one Mr Godfrey Hounsfield, an electrical engineer, who worked at an electromusical company (EMI).

I was bewildered at the news because I had not heard of this Hounsfield, even when I had been in England just a month earlier, but Dr Bull told me to expect something extraordinary. 'He's just drumming up a sense of drama to make sure the auditorium is full,' I thought to myself. Anyway, I duly went to attend the lecture and, after Mr Hounsfield had been introduced, he rose from his seat and turned to the machine on the stage to show the images.

To a stunned audience, in pin drop silence, he demonstrated his invention: the computed axial tomography or CT scanner of the head, which revolutionized neuro-imaging. Thunderous applause erupted. The audience rose as one to give a standing ovation. The sound of cameras clicking was deafening. Then there was a strange minute or two of silence as the truth of what had just been demonstrated began to sink in. It was the first time the human brain had been imaged. With the possible exception of Röntgen, the discoverer of the X-ray, Hounsfield's stupendous invention virtually changed the entire face of medical science, both in the domain of diagnosis and therapeutic interventions. As I looked in awe at the intracranial soft tissues and ventricles in the brain, seen as separate structures. I thought, 'This has turned medicine inside out. The practice of medicine will change forever. The Röntgen era is over. It was now the Hounsfield era.'

It was a moment I have never forgotten.

The invention earned Hounsfield a Nobel Prize in 1979 as well as many other awards and recognitions. The CT scanner is recognized by many as one of the top revolutionary advances in medicine, alongside the discovery of penicillin.

Hounsfield had worked for the famous EMI company and well-known record label on developing guided weapon systems and radar. While at EMI, he also developed an interest in computers. But the company started losing interest in Hounsfield's projects. His supervisors enquired whether he had anything to pursue. He said he had been toying with the idea of developing a computer software to compile X-rays of an object from various angles and organize them into a three-dimensional representation to help physicians to see the inside of the human body. The British Department of Health and Social Services could foresee some future in the project and provided him with a grant, and within a few years, Hounsfield designed and constructed a CT scanner in collaboration with two radiologists, James Ambrose and Louis Kreel in 1971, under the aegis of EMI. A test machine was later introduced at the Atkinson Morley Hospital in Wimbledon.

The device was first tested on preserved human brains; brains preserved in formalin. But the brains were not ideal because the chemical had hardened their tissues so severely that they no longer resembled normal brain matter. So, cow brains were procured from the local butcher's shop. These too had a problem, in that because an electric shock was used to stun the animals before they were slaughtered, this filled the brain with blood and the fluid obstructed the radiologists' view of the organ's structure. In the end, kosher cow brains were used because, instead of being stunned, the animals had their jugulars slit. The process drained blood away from the skull, which enabled clear CT scans of the brain.

In September 1971, a CT scanning machine was introduced into medical practice with the documentation of a cerebral cyst in a participant at Atkinson Morley Hospital. All this from a man who had no degree in medicine.

EMI began manufacturing CT scanners and sold them to hospitals with success. The machine had a mini-computer attached to it, which allowed doctors to scan 14 patients in an eight-hour day. But within five years, GEC, Siemens and Philips and other companies began making more enhanced, full-body scanners. EMI eventually stopped producing its scanners because it couldn't compete with the other established manufacturers.

After I saw Hounsfield's presentation, with delight, I thought thank God we can consign to the dustbin now the more aggressive, cumbersome and invasive procedures we used to visualize cerebral pathology or detect structural lesions in the brain. The CT was going to lead to an unprecedented advancement in the diagnosis of various ailments. Of that I was sure when, reeling from the unbelievable images I had seen, I was determined there and then that I would have to acquire a CT scanner for my department.

Also at Massachusetts General Hospital, I came across my first ultrasound machine. Ultrasound, often referred to as medical sonography, is the use of ultra-high-frequency sound waves for medical procedures. Although Scottish obstetrician Ian Donald created the first ultrasound in 1958, the technology goes back to Jacques and Pierre Curie in 1877. In 1958, Dr Ian Donald used this technology to observe the growth of foetuses in the womb to visualize abnormalities during pregnancy. X-rays are generally not used to image a foetus because of the potential harm radiation exposure can cause to the developing baby, especially during the early stages of pregnancy when the foetus's cells are rapidly dividing.

Donald's interest in ultrasound technology began when he met the director of a boiler fabrication company. The company used an industrial ultrasound to check for cracks in their welds. Donald was curious to know if the ultrasound could differentiate between different types of tissue. He visited the plant in 1955, bringing with him fibroids and a large ovarian cyst. He used the ultrasound machine on these tissue samples, comparing them with a steak as a control.

The experiment confirmed the machine's ability to scan biological tissue. Along with other contributors, Donald built a smaller version of the ultrasound to use on women expecting babies. The modern-day ultrasound machine expands beyond obstetrics though, and can effectively visualize most parts of the body, including the heart, blood vessels and abdomen.

While I was working in the experimental lab in the Mass General Hospital I met an assistant professor of the department, Dr Smith. 'Since you're experimenting, let me tell you that a new gadget called ultrasound has arrived in the department and is lying in the basement. Can you go and try twisting the knobs to see if any images are produced?'

Since I was free, with no specific responsibility, I went down to the basement and twisted some knobs, with no results. After a while, Dr Smith also came down. 'Listen, no one here knows what to do with this machine,' he said. 'If you want to learn how to use this new imaging device that is non-ionizing and uses ultrasound as an imaging source, you'd better go to Denmark.'

In short, at this time, no one in the USA knew about ultrasound but they knew about it in Denmark. I took Dr Smith's advice and contact and flew to Copenhagen when I got the chance in 1980 in my search for more knowledge about a non-ionizing source of imaging that was cheaper than a CT scan. My destination was Herlev Hospital, about two hours' drive from Copenhagen where Dr Henrik Holm taught me all about ultrasound scanning, enough to inspire me to feel determined to fly back home and introduce this new technique to patients at AIIMS. But before returning to India, I finished my tour by spending time in England, revisiting all the hospitals I had trained at some years earlier, such as the University College of Medicine, Middlesex Hospital, Brompton Hospital for Chest Diseases, Queen's Square Hospital for neuroradiology and Hammersmith Hospital for Cardiac Radiology.

———

At Copenhagen, I was almost flung into the entrance of the brand new Herlev Hospital – the gust of wind was so strong. It was 1980 or 1981 and the month of May, but it was very cold. I had two or three sweaters on top of my sari but was not wearing a protective hat. My head felt like a block of ice because of the high wind chill factor. As a child, one of my favourite books was a geography book called *Home's Far Away* about Scandinavia, and the images in it of Norway's fjords had made a powerful impression on me. It was a dream to visit Scandinavia, and here I was, spinning through the revolving door (or rather being propelled by the wind) – the first time I had seen one – into a brightly lit foyer where Dr Henrik Holm welcomed me, all bright-eyed and eager.

8

Building Up the Radiology Department Against the Cynics

I was so excited on my first day back at AIIMS, flushed with excitement over everything I had seen, that I almost skipped into the office. My first appeal was to the director of AIIMS and the officials of the ministry of health. Before meeting members of the bureaucracy, I fine-tuned my argument for the funds to buy a CT scanner and ultrasound machine to rebut what I knew they were going to say: *India is too poor a country to afford such advanced technology.*

My argument was this: India was full of paradoxes and contradictions. We had a space programme and an atomic energy board while food was transported in bullock carts from villages with no roads; we had many rich people and also some of the poorest; although the majority of our health problems were preventable and cheap to tackle, such as polio, tuberculosis, pneumonia and diarrhoea, we had chosen to develop a high-end healthcare centre like AIIMS. The solution was that just as basic health issues were being treated, in parallel we also had to treat more complicated ones with the best available technology in the world. Otherwise, we would always be left behind.

'We are providing funds for buying jets to transport 100–300 travellers at a time for pleasure and vacations but not willing to provide updated equipment for the healthcare for millions who need it?' I said in one meeting. 'Please give me the funds to buy a CT scanner and ultrasound machine to upgrade the healthcare of the nation. AIIMS was created by Parliament to be a centre of excellence and a model for the country. We must continue our mission.'

It was unrealistic to expect civil servants with no knowledge of medicine to understand the vast difference a CT scanner and ultrasound machine would make to the practice of medicine. Worse, if the request for funds was emanating from a 'back processing' department like radiology, it was unlikely to fall on receptive ears. But what could I do? I had no powerful patients with whom I had direct contact that would allow me to persuade them to plead my cause with bureaucrats. I was not friends with any politicians. Nor did I have any selling skills. And I was a woman.

Since my colleagues Professor Dr N. Gopinath, chief of cardiovascular surgery, and Professor P.N. Tandon, chief of neurosurgery, were going to be those who would most benefit from the new technology, I decided to collar them. (Professor Tandon's brother was joint secretary to the PM, which would also help.) They were skilled surgeons with good reputations. More importantly, some of them had treated civil servants and political leaders or their relatives and had occasions to socialize with them. Through these personal interactions, they might be able to collar someone useful to help me get funds. Without this kind of help, it was very unlikely that the health ministry, whose budget was a minuscule percentage of GDP, would give me the money I wanted.

Around this time, after they agreed to help me, we learnt that the Swedish International Development Agency was ready to give a grant of 30 million Swedish kroners. The economic affairs ministry had 13 projects competing for this grant. Dr Gopinath and Dr Tandon, who had both been working on obtaining funds for the creation of cardiovascular and neurosciences centres of excellence, wrote a report, backed by facts, and submitted it to the ministry. After considering all 13 projects, the ministry decided the AIIMS project was the most deserving and we were granted funds to buy a CT scanner. The health ministry paid for an ultrasound machine.

That day, I went home and thanked God in my prayers.

Before the magnificent machine even came, I got down to training the staff and here I tapped all the contacts I had made on my overseas trip. I invited Dr Torgny Greitz, chief of neuroradiology at the Karolinska Institute of Science in Stockholm, to visit us so that we could benefit from his experience as part of an exchange programme. I sent Dr R.K. Goulatia to Stockholm for further training in neuroradiology. Dr Tunnel, head of cardiovascular radiology at Karolinska, also visited us under the exchange programme.

In the department, I noticed that Dr N.K. Mishra, a senior resident, was good with his hands. It has to be said that not all residents are good with their hands. He quickly acquired the skills of arterial punctures (putting a needle into an artery) as well as vascular and non-vascular interventions (putting needles into blood vessels). I encouraged him to build his skills and teach the junior residents. When the learning curve was over, he developed exceptional interventional skills and became a real asset. No other radiology department in the country could boast of the range and depth of skills and academic standards that we had created at that time. When Dr Goulatia returned from Stockholm, we laid the foundation of neuroradiology at AIIMS and cut the umbilical cord from the general department.

As for the CT scanner, GEC in England was the only company manufacturing it at that time. The first five had been shipped to well-known neurological centres across the world, including Sweden. Thanks to our Swedish grant, GEC shipped out one scanner to us in 1978 (it was not the sixth) and was also kind enough to provide a service engineer who would collaborate with the Computer Management Corporation Private Limited so that the machine was carefully installed and rigorously maintained. The engineer was an Indian employed by GEC in London. Our Central Public Works Department (CPWD) laid out the infrastructure needed to install the CT scanner but treated the assignment as though they were building a latrine.

The 'installation' essentially meant the electrical wiring. The voltage and the current had to be very precise, far more than was required for X-rays, and the wiring had to be copper, not the aluminium used in homes.

The Public Works Department (PWD) team used aluminium electrical wiring instead of the stipulated copper wiring and used totally useless dust door sealers to keep the dust out. Very soon, we had our first breakdown. Our service engineer was at a loss for what needed to be done. General Electric Company sent a senior engineer from England who collapsed in a chair with shock when he saw the state of affairs. I wanted the ground to swallow me up when he unpacked a dust detecting machine. It broke into loud whining, indicating massive amounts of dust in the CT scanner and in the room and just would not stop. I realized that running high-technology medicine in low-technology countries was not going to be easy. But I had learnt my lesson. Henceforth, we gave a turnkey contract to all vendors and kept the CPWD out.

Our CT scanner was the only one not just in India but also in South Asia. Word spread that we were offering earlier, improved, non-traumatic and non-interventional diagnosis for our patients. Requests began coming in from hospitals in Nepal, Bhutan, Sri Lanka and Bangladesh who wanted to send their patients to us. At the end of the year, we analysed our data and published it in the *Indian Journal of Radiology* for the benefit of our local fraternity to encourage them to upgrade their services and acquire the technology now available.

It was also becoming clear, with reference to cardiovascular radiology, that the disease pattern in the cardiac sciences was

Inauguration of the CT Scanner by President of India Sanjiva Reddy, with a representative of GEC on the left and Prof Ramalinga Swami on the right, and with me explaining in the centre

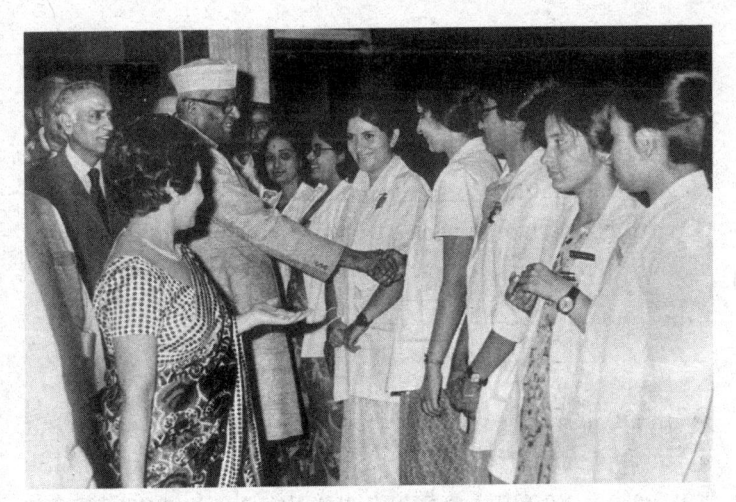

Introducing the faculty to President Sanjiva Reddy after the inauguration

changing from rheumatic heart disease (when the heart valves are permanently damaged by rheumatic fever) to ischaemic heart disease (when the heart muscle doesn't receive enough blood and oxygen) and congenital heart disease. Our skills had to expand to cope. I sent Dr Mira Rajani for a year to New Zealand to learn the new advances in ischaemic and congenital heart disease. On her return, she formed the basis of the section of cardiovascular radiology and subspecialization within the faculty and ultimately cut the umbilical cord from the general department.

Dr Sima Mukherjee took up chest diseases as well as the study of the interstitium of the lungs, the thin tissue space located between the tiny air sacs (alveoli) in the lungs. For paediatric radiology, I homed in on Dr Arun Gupta, who was gentle with children. He developed the specialty to a national level and rose to be the head of the department later on. Cancer was another area that was growing clinically. Dr Karan Singh was health minister then and, with the help of the Rotary Club, he built the Institute Rotary Cancer Hospital (IRCH). Specific clinical faculty was recruited but for radiology, predictably, no extra faculty was allotted. So, I started sending a senior resident for routine reporting and they could come to the main department. When they faced any difficulty in diagnosis I was always there to help them.

With a CT scanner in place, the next thing I did was to put in an application for an ultrasound machine with AIIMS's Purchase Committee. I heard later that the Committee was incredulous with one person on it saying:

'Has she gone mad? She's been allotted Rs 54 lakh for a CT scanner from the Swedish grant now she wants another Rs 4 lakh for an ultrasound!'

With that, they threw my application in the dustbin without informing me.

I understood that every department at AIIMS was fighting for money that was limited but I persisted and eventually, we were able to buy our first ultrasound machine, made by Siemens. But it encountered the usual initial resistance. At a meeting of the Indian Radiological and Imaging Association, a speaker showed a prenatal X-ray diagnosis of osseous diseases. At the end of his lecture, he received warm applause. When it died down, I rose from my seat on to the stage and said that, with ultrasound now available – which is non-ionizing radiation – we cannot continue to teach and demonstrate X-rays of pregnant mothers that exposed mother and foetus to radiation.

I was booed as loudly as the speaker was cheered.

'This is not AIIMS!' one person shouted.

'We're a poor country! We can't afford ultrasound machines,' said another.

I was furious and shouted back, 'We cannot be teaching the next generation what Röntgen discovered in 1895. We have to move forward for the next generation, not show techniques that were used in the 1960s!'

I walked off the stage to even louder booing and jeering.

I spent a fair amount of time urging clinicians in various subspecialties to take up the ultrasound. X-rays could only show the chest, bones and abdomen. They could not show the liver, spleen, kidney or bladder unless you injected a patient with a contrast dye, which ran the risk of an anaphylactic shock, a severe allergic reaction that could be fatal. The ultrasound images could give urologists, nephrologists and gastroenterologists vastly more information than an X-ray. The

When I was elected as President of the Indian Radiological Association, 1982

At the First US–India Radiology Conference

new machines helped enormously in changing how radiology was viewed. It commanded more respect. It had become mainstream. Moreover, CT scanners covering the whole body had developed, and I was sanctioned funds to buy one.

Meanwhile, someone with no link to AIIMS was working to bring CT scanners to India. One Mr Gupta, an entrepreneur who had a computer business, had gone to the USA to have his ailing wife treated, and at the end of her stay, he noticed one very expensive item on the bill. He asked what the 'CT scanner' was and, on being told, made inquiries and found a firm in the USA near bankruptcy because its machines were not of the same quality as those made by GEC or Siemens. The company told Mr Gupta he could have the whole lot at a throwaway price. He bought them and shipped them to India to install them in some state capitals and Tier 2 cities. Though these scanners were not high quality, they were adequate to help neurosurgeons decide, in cases of trauma and vascular anomalies, whether to surgically intervene or not. They also helped to confirm brain tumours and other space-occupying lesions in a non-invasive fashion, which was a huge benefit. The small-town hospitals were happy with the scanners. I applauded the move as it pushed smaller hospitals up the learning curve and to the standards being set at AIIMS.

Around the same time, Dr Arjun Das Sehgal, neurosurgeon and consultant at Sir Ganga Ram Hospital in Delhi, also acquired a CT scanner and offered our department's Dr Meera Rao a job with a very handsome salary. I was sorry to lose her but was cognizant of the fact that, in a way, it was our role to create and train manpower and teachers for the country so that they could elevate medical services and create jobs.

The problem was, and still is, the shortage of radiologists. There is a mismatch. On the one hand, India must treat all the legacy diseases, such as TB and malaria, while simultaneously tackling a whole raft of new chronic conditions such as diabetes and heart disease along with strokes and cancer. With technology advancing, radiologists are not only facing an increase in the volume of imaging owing to the greater number of scans being carried out but also an increase in the number of images per scan. The demand will only increase as chronic diseases become more prevalent and the size of the elderly population continues to grow. It is estimated that India has approximately 20,000 radiologists as of 2024 to serve a population of over 1.4 billion people. This translates to a ratio of one radiologist for every 100,000 individuals, far below the levels of other countries.

Consequently, patients are forced to wait for long periods for imaging tests, adding to their anxiety and delaying diagnosis. I am firmly convinced that telemedicine and technology generally, including AI, will provide solutions for the fact that we neither have enough radiologists and nor are training them in greater numbers. Irrespective of location, scans can be reviewed and patients can be diagnosed. There is, of course, talk that AI will take over the job of radiologists and do it better. I am not in a position to challenge or accept this prediction but certainly, in the short term, it will increase radiologists' efficiency and productivity. Most certainly, technology is the only way to bridge the chasm between urban and rural India because no trained radiologist (even if there were lots of them) is going to relocate from a city to the countryside.

My parents, 1928

Sacred Heart Convent, Dalhousie, 1939. I am first from the left in the front row.

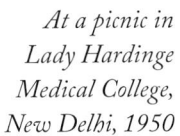

At a picnic in Lady Hardinge Medical College, New Delhi, 1950

As president of the students union, I am leading Health Minister Rajkumari Amrit Kaur and Vice President Sarvepalli Radhakrishnan, 1952.

My family, with my grandparents at the centre, 1952. My father is behind his father and my mother is by his side.

My husband and I after the jaimala, *1959*

Being awarded the fellowship of the National Academy of Medical Sciences (NAMS) by Justice M.C. Chagla, the Chief Justice of India

Being received by my predecessor as director of AIIMS, 1984

Being introduced to Prince Charles, now King Charles III

With Dr Malik, the director general of the WHO, Geneva, and Dr Koko, the director general of the WHO, Southeast Asia, in my office at AIIMS, 1985

Dancing after being appointed as president of the Indian Radiological Association, 1982

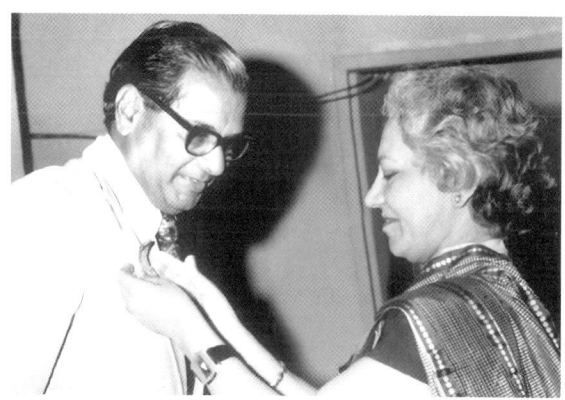

Handing over charge to my successor at the Indian Radiological Association, 1983

After being elected as president of the Indian Radiological Association, 1982

Inauguration of the linear accelerator by President A.P.J. Abdul Kalam at Dharamshila Cancer Hospital

With Dr Karan Singh, the then health minister

Receiving the Lifetime Achievement Award from Prime Minister Atal Bihari Vajpayee at the International Society of Radiology (ISR) conference in New Delhi, 1998

Receiving the Padma Shri from President Shri R. Venkataraman, 1991

Receiving the Lifetime Achievement Award from Prime Minister Narendra Modi, 2014

Receiving an honorary membership of the Radiological Society of North America (RSNA) from Dr Vijay Rao, 2018

Four generations in one image – my mother, myself, my son and granddaughter

My family on my mother's eightieth birthday

My family at my son and daughter-in-law's twenty-fifth wedding anniversary

With Abhishek Bhartia after the CT scanner was installed at Sitaram Bhartia Institute of Science and Research

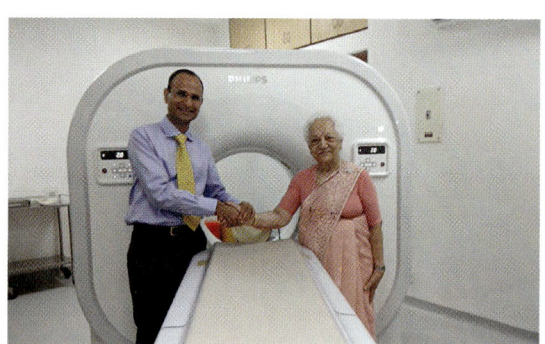

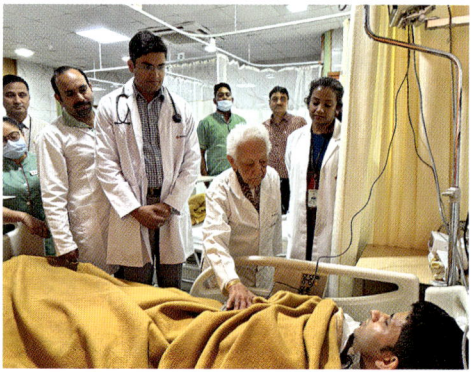

With doctors and nurses on my rounds at Sitaram Bhartia Institute of Science and Research

9

Director of AIIMS

In 1977, a very controversial appointment happened. Dr Lalit Prakash Agarwal, chief of ophthalmology, was appointed as dean of AIIMS. He was good at his job, and he is credited for setting up the Rajendra Prasad Centre for Ophthalmic Sciences at AIIMS in 1967, when he was only 45 years old. As a proud Indian, he was distressed to see so many Indians go abroad for eye treatment. He was determined to make India self-reliant in the field of ophthalmology. In 1976, he drafted what is known today as the National Programme for Control of Blindness, the first of its kind in the world. Dr Agarwal's contributions to modern Indian ophthalmology prompted some to call him 'the father of modern Indian ophthalmology'.

As a person, I found him obnoxious, and he was widely disliked for being fiercely ambitious, egotistical, quarrelsome, abrasive and vindictive. As one my colleagues said, 'His personality is such that he is unhappy when peace prevails and very happy to create unrest.' He instilled fear in the staff at every level. He had no idea how to treat people with courtesy. 'I'm the boss, you're a nobody,' was the message his body language conveyed.

In 1979, when a new director was due to be appointed and Dr Agarwal was mentioned as a top contender, a wave of unrest swept over the campus. When the health secretary came for a radiological examination one day, I seized the opportunity to express the reservations most of us felt about Dr Agarwal. Not knowing Dr Agarwal's dictatorial nature, he airily dismissed my concern with a wave of the hand. I had failed to convey the sense of dread prevailing in AIIMS. Yes, Dr Agarwal was a good strategist, organizer and a visionary. But he was not director material. The selection committee went ahead and chose him.

Since he wanted to prove that all his predecessors had been hopeless and unable to leave a good legacy and that only he could raise AIIMS to an exalted status, Dr Agarwal trashed everyone else's work, trying to dig out irregularities in well-run departments such as radiology, neurosurgery and paediatric surgery, both in patient care and accounts. Having failed in this, he tried to provoke differences among senior colleagues within departments as well as inter-departmentally. He would take an assistant professor aside and tell him that his boss thought his work was rubbish. Or he would tell a senior surgeon in one department that another top surgeon in another department had belittled his skills. The stirring up of envy and resentment was endless.

A few weeks after he took over, Dr Agarwal asked me to take over as chair of the Hospital Management Board. Why me? I was not likely to pull any political and bureaucratic strings against him, having none. But I never refused any responsibility, whether it was voluntary training during the 1962 Sino-Indian War, or being part of the team that negotiated the setting up of a hospital in Churu, Rajasthan, or being professor in charge of the library.

The Hospital Management Board was created a long time ago, when we had failed to find a suitable senior administrator to serve as medical superintendent. A senior faculty member chaired the Board, in addition to their departmental duties. Unknowingly and unintentionally, Dr Agarwal gave me the opportunity to acquire valuable administrative experience over the next five years while continuing to be head of radiology.

Like everyone else, I kept my distance, avoiding meeting him. As with my radiology department, I have found that regular meetings keep everyone on their toes and reduce the chances of any slacking. As chair of the board, I took a physical round of the hospital every Thursday, followed by a meeting with supervisors of departments of nursing, maintenance staff, housekeeping and laundry, security and sterilization. This was the time when, if anyone needed guidance, it could be given.

I had no choice but to meet Dr Agarwal when a nurse shortage reached critical levels. You see, we were receiving more and more patients every day and our faculty was expanding but the number of nurses had not increased commensurately. Staff whose relatives had been admitted felt the problem acutely, and there was total agreement on the need to recruit more.

Except, that is, in the director's office. The nursing superintendent and I explained the problem to Dr Agarwal. 'You will never convince me you are short of nurses.' He was clearly unaware that the number of nurses needed in an eye operation was nothing compared to the number needed for cardiovascular or neurological surgery. We were building up the cardiac and neurosciences centres and needed more staff. We had data to prove our poor patient–nurse ratio but he was obdurate.

Only when a relative of a senior civil servant was admitted and complained about the nurse shortage did Dr Agarwal call me in and asked what ratio I wanted.

Luckily, he was soon to be fired and this is how it happened. The political scene in the country after Emergency was lifted in 1977 was lively. The unshackled media was active and probing every issue freely, including the troubled situation at AIIMS. Information was reaching Mrs Gandhi from many sources, including Professor Shantilal J. Mehta, a respected member of the Institute Body and later chairman of the Institute Review Committee. Professor Mehta was also personal surgeon to Mrs Gandhi who had great regard for him. At a meeting with Mrs Gandhi one evening, she asked why he was looking so downcast. 'The very pillars of the Institute are shaking,' he is reported to have said, or words to that effect. 'I am deeply disappointed and worried about AIIMS's future the way things are going under Agarwal and I believe something needs to be done urgently to prevent its collapse. The festering ill-will on the campus has crossed all limits.'

Two days later, Dr Agarwal received a letter informing him that a committee comprising five senior faculty members was to be set up and, until then, he should take no policy decision. This was a great personal insult to Dr Agarwal, who refused to heed the instruction. Faced with defiance, Mrs Gandhi told the health ministry to call for a governing body meeting and compulsorily retired Dr Agarwal. His tenure was for five years; he had completed about 10 months. Dr H.D. Tandon was appointed acting director, and a malevolent period at AIIMS came to an end. Dr Tandon continued as acting director until 1984, when I took over. I was a good administrator and ran a tight ship. While he was acting director, I continued working as professor of radiology in the radiology department in, I might add, a much more harmonious and collegial atmosphere than under Dr Agarwal.

One morning in early 1984 – I don't recollect when exactly – Mr Parija, who was the deputy director administration at the time, came to the radiology department to check some data that was required for Parliament questions.

'Have you applied for the director's job?' he asked, out of the blue.

'I haven't even thought about it because I've got so much on my hands.'

'You are number five in terms of seniority. Two of the senior faculty are not interested in applying. The other two are going to retire, so you are on the top of the list. You should apply.'

I was 54 years old. I had served AIIMS for 24 years. Apart from building up the radiology department, I had conducted extensive clinical research – studies in pulmonary hypertension in rheumatic heart disease, TB of the central nervous system (CNS), aortoarteritis, renal hypertension, gastrointestinal radiology and cardiovascular radiology to name a few. (The interested reader can find more details of my research in the appendix.)

I had six more years left before retirement. Mr Parija's words made me think. After discussing it with my husband and two retired directors, I decided to apply. The institute began to buzz with speculation, gossip and predictions about who the next director would be. As the date of the selection committee meeting grew nearer, the gossip mills went into a frenzy. My chief radiographer, Arjun Singh, who had worked with me for 24 years, told me that even the campus bus stops and the campus milk booth were full of talk. Who is going to get it? Who has the political connections? Which applicant has a 'godfather' in the bureaucracy? How will Dr Sneh Bhargava, a political babe-in-the-woods, leverage the political clout needed to land the most prestigious medical job in the country?

I had never cultivated any political lobby. I had no family background in political circles, I was hopeless at selling myself, and as a woman and mother, I had never gone around 'networking' to cultivate contacts that could be useful to me in my career. It was simply not something a woman could do without it being wildly misconstrued and even backfiring. Owing to the nature of radiology, I had hardly any direct contact with patients or politicians and their families who could pull strings or put in a word for me. We may provide a diagnosis to clinicians and guide them correctly, but the credit for it and the opportunity of follow-up always went to the clinician mainly.

Instead, I had focussed on discharging my responsibilities. Whoever was looking at my application would have to judge me based on my work. I had developed the radiology department from a back-office role into mainstream medicine and made it so frontline that our services were sought by every department for patient care, teaching and research. That was my record. In fact, my record had led to my being dubbed the 'Indira Gandhi of AIIMS'.

There were other applicants for the job who had plenty of political connections and had a very high opinion of themselves, but I turned out to be the only woman applicant. Today, the situation has changed immeasurably. At medical colleges, the sex ratio is around 50:50, but in those days the entire profession was male-dominated.

A call came from the office of the health minister, inviting me to meet him at his residence. As a political ingenue, I am not ashamed to admit I did not know his address. On walking in, he greeted me warmly. 'Mrs Gandhi has decided to put the responsibility of running AIIMS on your shoulders. The institute body will meet and formalize the necessary procedures.'

As chair of the Hospital Management Board, I had met Mrs Gandhi several times. She was perceptive and observant. I can only assume that she did not let any gender bias get in the way of selecting me for the honour.

I thanked the minister and pledged to look after the institute's reputation and to build on its legacy. AIIMS was a household name, a trusted brand, a byword for excellence. New departments were coming up on the campus: cardiothoracic, neurosciences, cancer and many others. The hospital had started with 10 departments in 1956. When I was formally appointed as director on 31 October 1984, the day Mrs Gandhi was assassinated, we had 45 departments and centres.

My mother was delighted with the news. 'Had my father been alive, he would have been euphoric,' she said. Their faith in my desire to become a doctor had been vindicated. As I have said earlier in this book, my parents encouraged me in my desire to become a doctor. It was not their wish; it was mine. I always knew they were behind me, my best cheerleaders. They understood my desire – a desire many people of my generation felt – to work towards making India the best we could make it. When I became an MD, my mother gave me a gift of five guineas. Whenever I received a pay rise, she gave me a gift. The drawback was that she spent the rest of her life being besieged by people's requests for help to get admission at AIIMS. She developed a very practised routine whenever anyone approached her. She used to raise her folded hands while they were still at a distance and say: 'Please do not ask me to do something that is not right. I will convey your request to Sneh and if she thinks she can do anything to help, she will call you.' Not everyone was pleased with this response.

The responsibility of leading one of the temples of modern India, as envisaged by Jawaharlal Nehru, was daunting. By now, in 1984, AIIMS was a quarter of a century old. There was a lustre to its name. There was only one AIIMS, renowned throughout India as a centre of medical excellence, a byword for the best doctors could offer and a lifeline for millions of underprivileged Indians. It functioned like a lodestar for Indians with few means or none at all. They packed a small bag and left their homes and farms in every corner of India to travel long distances by bus and by train in search of a cure, faithfully following the lodestar until it delivered them to the portals of the hospital where salvation awaited. Even today, *India Today*'s annual survey shows AIIMS to be the best hospital in the country.

Walk in any day and the vast halls and corridors are thronging with families bringing their sick ones to the only place they can trust. Even in the early days of AIIMS, before it had grown to vast proportions, we had taken a decision not to put out floor beds. It was not an easy decision. Some very sick people come, some in great pain and discomfort. But to have a patient on the floor was not acceptable to us. It was our responsibility to treat the patient with care, not to add indignity to their troubles. Studies have shown that undignified care can have an unfavourable impact on the patient's recovery, such as leading to depression and loss of will to live.

Yet it has never been easy to cope with the gigantic influx every day, with people lying outside on the road while they wait their turn all because successive governments were unable to build an AIIMS in every state capital – a reputed and trustworthy AIIMS – to serve the needs of an exploding population and to alleviate the impossible pressure on one institution.

Some of the saddest cases we saw were people whose disease could not be cured because it had advanced greatly due to their inability to afford a doctor's fee where they lived or the absence of a qualified doctor at their district hospital. Some of the most depressing images I have looked at in my career have been those where the cancer – whether in the breast, brain, lung or oral cavity – had advanced so far that it was inoperable. Advanced breast cancer used to be very common indeed. A devastating cocktail of ignorance, neglect by relatives and shyness about consulting a doctor about the lump the women felt meant that they came to me for X-rays too late in the day and the image was invariably one of a worst-case scenario tumour I dreaded – that of a 'rising sun', a round shadow with streaks all over it. Others I hated seeing were unexpected metastatic disease, foetal death in utero or serious findings needing immediate hospital admission.

In response to the great demand, the hospital had grown too, with more specialities and departments and ever more sophisticated research, a wider range of technology and a growing and diverse body of doctors whose skills had been honed and polished to a superlative level by sheer dint of the deep experience they gained from treating so many patients and diverse conditions.

AIIMS occupied a unique position. It could not be compared with any hospital in the West where the health budget varied from 5 to 13 per cent of the GDP compared to India's budget of 0.99–1 per cent of the GDP. Yet, despite the massive disparity in funding, patient care and surgical results were comparable to the best in the UK, Europe and the USA. The diseases of the West were different from ours, in that many of ours were preventable and caused by poor sanitation and lack of clean drinking water whereas many of theirs were lifestyle related.

In India, too, the disease profile was changing. As mentioned earlier, in the 1950s and '60s, rheumatic heart disease caused by a bacterial infection had been common but by now it was under control, while the leading heart disease was ischaemic heart disease or coronary heart disease due to poor lifestyle, incorrect diet and lack of exercise. Infectious diseases were fewer yet diseases peculiar to us such as leprosy and tuberculosis were still largescale.

As I walked through the doors on my first day as director, I felt a shudder of excitement and trepidation. It was my responsibility to build on the reputation and credibility of an institution for which many had worked with utter dedication.

This is my moment, this is my time to make a contribution towards the cause for which AIIMS was established and for which Mrs Gandhi has appointed me.

It would have to be both an individual and team effort to advance the cause that many of my predecessors had selflessly pursued.

I would not be here without the unflinching support of my husband and family.

Thank God Amar is my rock and that I can turn to him for advice if I face any obstacles.

At AIIMS, the academic faculty was directly involved in clinical practice, medical education and research. This synergy is unparalleled in other professions. The complex interdependence of these three functions is one of the hallmarks of academic medicine. AIIMS had to be run with integrity, truthfulness, compassion and accountability.

As the first woman director of AIIMS, it might have been expected that I would face a tremendous amount of opposition or ridicule in the patriarchal society that surrounded me. In fact, after 24 years at AIIMS, the faculty all knew me and my work and there was no question of gender discrimination. What I frequently encountered was incredulity externally. My secretary would put through calls from senior officials and even ministers who would be shocked on hearing a female voice as director.

'I'm sorry but I've been put through to the wrong number,' some would say. My response was to laugh it off and get down to the matter at hand.

Over the years, I was able to create numerous new departments: a centre for teaching, department of haematology and department of biotechnology. I also attempted to bring about department of emergency medicine and an international clinical epidemiology network.

An early crisis arose in the first few weeks of my directorship, as if the assassination of Mrs Gandhi were not crisis enough, when, coincidentally, three out of the four professors of surgery at AIIMS left, two to join hospitals in the Middle East and one to join the World Health Organization (WHO). That left only Dr Samiran Nundy, a gastroenterology surgeon, who was the youngest of them all and he was an associate professor, not a professor. I was, frankly, very jittery. How would we cope with surgeries with only one senior surgeon? And rumours were swirling that Dr Nundy too was planning to leave for the Middle East.

'I hear you want to leave but I can't possibly let you go,' I told Dr Nundy after calling him into my office. 'What do you want?'

'For me to stay, I'd have to be given my own department of gastroenterology surgeon,' he said.

I knew he was a good surgeon and deserved to be a professor too but Dr B.M.L. Kapoor was a general surgeon and, since most of a general surgeon's work is abdominal, he obviously would not want a separate department of gastroenterology as it would hive off most of his work. I called Dr Kapoor as I had to find a solution that was acceptable to both men and explained that we could not possibly let Dr Nundy go. If we gave him the department he wanted, we could make sure he was confined to certain kinds of surgery while Dr Kapoor would continue with the rest and the 'rest' would be considerable. To my mind, this seemed the only solution.

A few days later, I heard that the National Association of Surgeons of India had agreed to Dr Kapoor's request to create a separate section for gastroenterology surgeons throughout Indian hospitals.

'Is this true Dr Kapoor?' I asked. 'Because if so, thank you for throwing the solution into my lap. We can go ahead with Dr Nundy having a department of gastroenterology surgery and your department can be called the department of surgical disciplines.' Dr Nundy took his department up to new levels of achievement and success. Not only did he elevate his speciality, he also invited the editor of the *British Medical Journal* to hold a workshop at AIIMS on medical writing and data collection. Later, he was instrumental in the setting up of the *National Medical Journal of India* in 1988 as its founding editor-in-chief, and the peer-reviewed journal has remained highly respected to this day.

Once this was resolved, my next major task was to address the pressing issue of housing for AIIMS staff as suggested by my predecessor.

After the welcoming ceremonies and handover, I sat down with my predecessor Dr Tandon over a cup of tea and discussed what lay ahead of me. 'What, Dr Tandon, are the three immediate problems that need to be addressed urgently?' I asked.

'Housing, housing and housing,' he replied. 'The staff numbers now have far outstripped the housing available on the campus over 28 years. The residences for doctors and staff were built with the expectation of average growth but our growth has been phenomenal, far beyond our expectations.'

More housing was indeed a critical issue. It was imperative for housing to be nearby and easily accessible for the sake of comfort, for the sake of a work–life balance, but also because our staff provided a 24/7 service and needed to be available quickly for patients at any point. It was in dealing with this issue that I realized that, as director, my job was now very different from handling a department and would perforce involve knocking my head against many walls: politicians, vested interests, unresponsive civil servants, red tape, internal disagreement at AIIMS itself and their numerous intersections, often with uncertain results.

'Don't we have land behind the gents hostel which we could use to build more homes?' I asked Dr Tandon.

'Yes, but the land is occupied by jhuggis.'

Let me meet the local MLAs to see how the residents of the jhuggi can be relocated, I thought.

Little did I know in my naivete that this would be a hornet's nest. When I met the MLA and suggested relocation, he looked stunned. 'Dr Bhargava, do you want us to lose the election by dismantling the jhuggis?' I explained that it was the hospital's land and we needed space for more housing but I had to beat a hasty retreat. This was one door it would not be easy to pry open, at least not yet.

Trying to approach the issue from another angle, I went to meet the vice chairman of the Delhi Development Authority (DDA) since it was the body that had allotted the land to us. Feigning cooperation, the chairman asked me how many jhuggis needed to be moved. After consulting the estate officer and the security officer, I was able to give him a figure. Later, I came to know that the security officer and estate officer were hand-in-glove with the jhuggiwallas and they had given me bogus data.

After months of efforts, the day finally came for the moving of the settlement and the DDA teams arrived with their tractors. Since protests might erupt, I was advised to leave the campus. When the tractor operator saw the number of jhuggis he had to contend with, he backed off as it was a far greater number than he had been told. The operation was called off.

A second operation was going to cost Rs 10,000 per jhuggi to relocate them and there was a whole row of them. We did not have this kind of budget. In those days, we were still living hand to mouth. I decided to take out a bank loan, and for this I needed the approval of the Planning Commission and the finance ministry. It transpired that the Act of Parliament under which AIIMS was created does not provide for taking loans. Who on earth was going to start the process of amending the Act? Who was going to run around from one ministry to another? Instead, we decided to wait for a while. By 31 March, all state governments had to tell the centre what funds they have not been able to spend in the financial year and return it to the centre. At that point, we would tell the health ministry about our need for extra money to clear the jhuggis for housing. When the time came, we were granted what we needed.

I informed the DDA that it could start relocating the jhuggis and we would pay. On the appointed day, the DDA tractors came again and started their work. After a while, the work stopped. The lieutenant governor had issued a stay order and he could not be contacted because he was travelling by road and no mobile phones were available in those days. Later, he told me that he had come under pressure from the MLA to issue the stay order.

The jhuggis continued to stand, taunting me. As in the past, when an obstacle refused to budge, I began looking for my favourite and reliable lever, that is, was there anyone who had been operated on or treated by our doctors? When pressure was applied at this sensitive point, I found that the obstacle usually obliged. It turned out that our gastroenterology surgeon, Dr Samiran Nundy, had operated on the MLA who was obstructing us. Our deputy director of administration appealed to Dr Nundy to speak to the MLA. Dr Nundy refused, saying he did not ask patients for favours. I was abroad at the time, but my colleagues tried to impress on Dr Nundy that this was not a personal favour we were asking but the simple return of that which belonged to AIIMS.

Mercifully, Dr Nundy understood the wider point and came around. Put on the spot by a request from Dr Nundy who had cured his relative, the MLA relented. We reassured him that the jhuggi residents would not be left homeless. We had found land elsewhere for them and also arranged electricity and water connections. The MLA was unimpressed and bitter. 'Well, that's no good to me because that area isn't my constituency, is it?' he replied.

Our doctors and staff prepared meals at their homes for the jhuggi residents and brought them to the campus to be distributed by the administrative staff as they knew that the jhuggi residents, in the relocation process, would be unable to cook. In fact, we also provided treatment to some of the residents, which won us some goodwill. I recall the strange case of a middle-aged man from the jhuggi who had extreme anaemia: a haemoglobin of 2 mg when the normal is 15–16 mg. A clinical diagnosis to see if there was carcinoma anywhere in the gastrointestinal tract was necessary. I started the study and suspected a tumour.

Given his extreme anaemia, I concluded it was a carcinoma of the stomach and sent a report accordingly. No other abnormality was detected in the rest of the bowel and the surgeon decided to operate. On the day of the operation, I received a call from the operation theatre to go up. I went, thinking they had found a huge tumour. Instead, I saw a bowl of teeming hookworms the size of the mass I had seen on the X-ray. Some were on the surgeon's hands and some were crawling all over the sterilized sheet.

After the initial shock, we all laughed, relieved that the man did not have a malignant tumour. The operation theatre staff changed their clothes and sterilized the room. Had it been a single hookworm I would have realized what it was, but because they were massed together in one big lump, I interpreted the mass as a tumour. Later, I published an article, 'Pitfalls in the Diagnosis of Carcinoma of the Stomach'.

Gradually, through persuasion and goodwill, it was agreed that the jhuggis would be dismantled. The tractors did their job, and much later when we had funds, we built facilities on the vacated land. The whole experience was salutary for me. Whatever the issue was, I could count on confronting an intricate web of vested interests which were hard to break though. The only possible route to success was for us to work as a team with one purpose.

Meanwhile, I read in the media that Prime Minister Rajiv Gandhi was allotting flats in Asiad Village, near AIIMS, to teachers and artists. I could not miss this opportunity to acquire some flats for our faculty. But how to get to the Prime Minister? There was no relative or political figure of his who needed treatment at AIIMS. That meant he was unlikely to be visiting any time soon. Going through the proper bureaucratic channels would take forever, by which time the flats would have been allotted.

I had to come up with something quickly. An epiphany duly obliged. The PM's daily durbar, of course. I turned up at Mr Gandhi's residence and stood in line along with hundreds of other supplicants. Why not? It meant access, if I was lucky, and a chance to appeal to him directly, face to face. The line moved slowly, inch by inch. I shuffled along with everyone else. Mr Gandhi made his way down the line until he drew close to me and did a double take.

'Doctor Bhargava, what on earth are you doing here?'

'Mr Prime Minister, I hear you are going to allot Asiad Village flats to teachers and artists. My faculty are also both teachers and artists, and we are in acute need of flats for staff who work 24x7. We don't have enough flats for them on the campus, so I am here to plead with you to allot 100 flats to us. Coming here was the only way I could reach you and make a request without a delay.'

He asked his aide for a notepad and pen and wrote, '100 flats allotted to AIIMS'.

Turning to me, he said, 'Go and see Sarla ji, my principal secretary, and she will do the needful.'

I thanked him profusely and rushed off with the precious paper, to give it to Sarla Grewal who, incidentally, was the former secretary of health and understood the service AIIMS was fulfilling.

'I will put this through but it will be processed through the health ministry, so you need to follow up with them,' Grewal told me.

After returning from a WHO meeting in Geneva, I was chagrined to hear the health ministry had halved the number of flats to 50. I felt like fighting the decision but thought better of it. Since I had not gone through the health ministry, it was very unlikely to reverse its decision. I settled for 50 and moved on.

What happened next was utterly unexpected. When I cheerfully made the announcement to senior faculty, thinking they would be thrilled with the Asiad Village flats, they refused to move out of the AIIMS campus to the flats, even though they were brand new.

'The accommodation here is so close we can walk to work whereas if we move to Asiad Village, we will have to arrange transport because we don't have our own cars. That's going to mean an extra cost on our already low salaries,' one doctor explained.

In the end, we allotted the 50 flats to junior faculty. They had no cars of their own so we hired a coach and later bought our own to bring the faculty to and from Asiad Village. I was pleased, having partially solved the critical housing problem and created an asset for AIIMS.

Dealing with discontented staff anywhere is a challenge but at AIIMS there was always an extra element, in that politicians were constantly on the lookout for a chance to interfere and throw their weight around in order to feel important. Those who were on various committees sometimes appointed people unsuited to the job who would do the politicians' bidding. Every single director of AIIMS had to learn to handle this constant tension between politicians who had the power and people running AIIMS who understood what the Institute needed and had a vision for the future.

Sometimes interference was instigated by doctors who curried favour with politicians to gain something in return. When the Assam chief minister's brother met with an accident in the state, the chief minister approached New Delhi for a chest surgeon to be sent. The brother needed to have a tube inserted into his lungs to drain the blood that had collected there to help relieve pressure on the lungs. At that time, I had only one chest surgeon at AIIMS because chest surgery had become unfashionable, replaced by cardiac surgery. At the behest of the health ministry, I sent my one chest surgeon to Assam. He inserted the tube, the lung expanded and the patient felt better. But instead of returning, the surgeon stayed on in Assam, ingratiating himself with the chief minister with a specific goal in mind. I realized what the goal was when I received an order to promote him, a lecturer, to professor. The Assam chief minister had written to Delhi praising the chest surgeon and asked for his elevation.

I called him in and blasted him. 'Who do you think you are? You don't deserve to be a professor whether by age or experience. Do you think I am going to pass over those who are more deserving than you?'

Of course, I refused to promote him, and within a year, he left AIIMS. But the point I am making is that there was often mutual back-scratching going on between politicians and some doctors – only some – with each party hoping to benefit. If a doctor pandered to a politician, the hope was for some appointment on a panel, committee or university, which would lead to travel and emoluments.

At any given moment, three politicians were on the Institute Body, itching to meddle. The Institute Body comprised 10 members who look after different areas, such as academics, selection, finances, etc. Politicians were members of three areas and had no need of any particular qualification to become a member. They were particularly keen on heading the selections committee as that gave them an opportunity to choose their favourites.

The campus was already a lively and fractious place. We had an active class 4 union, a super-active resident doctors' union and a faculty association. Whenever they got a whiff of any conflict, the politicians – even the small fry – always knew someone or another on the faculty and were quick to fish in troubled waters.

When my deputy director's term was about to end, I decided on Sunita Mukherjee, a member of the Himachal Pradesh cadre who had served in Nurpur and Solan and who enjoyed the support of the chief minister. The deputy director was always an IAS officer, not a doctor. Sunita had broken several glass ceilings. She had served as the MD of the State Electronic Corporation, and now that Rajiv Gandhi was ushering in computers, I wanted to tap Sunita's expertise in computerizing the hospital. I had attended some computer classes but was otherwise clueless about how to proceed.

When she arrived from Shimla, Sunita soon realized what a busy place AIIMS was and how demanding the staff were. Doctors who have been working for 24 hours are furious if the food has finished. Overworked students yell if they want ice cream and find there isn't any. Endless VIP visits had to be managed. You had to make a fuss over the person and the entourage. Sunita was constantly running from one meeting to another. 'I've started sleeping in my salwar kameez, it's faster that way instead of changing in a rush and reaching the site before you,' she told me one day. I understood her point. Every day, the work was so completely consuming, there was no time to think of anything else. On top of all her responsibilities, I asked her to handle the computerization of AIIMS in the administrative areas and patient records. Whenever it was time to issue tenders, you could be sure that the chair of the selection committee would assert his or her power or insist on a person of his or her choosing to take on a role, in this case, to head the computer section, and also in this case, a totally undesirable choice.

'I will have my way on this,' he told me. 'And then I will allow you to appoint other faculty on merit.'

By now, I had learnt to choose which battles to fight. I let him have this one.

But another battle was brewing. The PhD students went on strike over their demand for an additional stipend. The government refused to play ball. We had orders from the court that those on strike must not disturb patients or the smooth running of the hospital, but of course they did, as it was the only way they could attract attention. Later, they went on hunger strike and were serious. After a few days, their health began deteriorating. We were forced to force-feed them. Sunita had to go to the High Court to get an injunction asking for the protest to be moved outside onto the street as it was interfering with patient care. Kapil Sibal was the famous lawyer representing the students, and he happened to be Sunita's class fellow in senior school. She walked across to him, and when asked why he was on the opposing side, he supposedly replied, 'I work for whoever can afford my fees.'

She represented the hospital in court herself. As part of the injunction the court granted us, the striking students were told: no slogan-mongering within 500 yards of the hospital.

In a tense atmosphere, Sunita and I decided we had to create more camaraderie and mutual understanding. We began a series of cultural programmes for the staff to alleviate the stress and make sure it was not all work and no play. This helped release some of the pressure that tended to build up and also served to keep political interference at bay – by keeping our own house in order, there was less pretext for politicians to meddle. Sunita also selected what she called vigilance staff, who would report to her if they heard of strikes or protests being planned so that we would not be taken by surprise. It also meant we could confront problems while they were still embryonic. Sunita and I presented a good strong team, the two of us, as we both thought alike, so much so that on occasion cries of '*Ma beti ka raj nahi chalega* (The mother–daughter rule is unacceptable)' were heard. To which we responded with, 'Come to us with your problems and we will solve them together. *Isliye ma beti ka raj hi chalega.*'

Resisting the demands of officials in the health ministry could be tedious. The deputy minister of health, on one occasion, became decidedly hostile when she wanted me to make her a member of the Institute Body and I had to tell her that it was not possible.

'Ma'am, we are guided by an Act of Parliament, and I have no powers to make you a member.'

She was miffed. 'You will not do it because you do not wish to do it.'

A few months later, a relative of hers met with a car accident and was admitted to Narender Mohan Hospital in Ghaziabad with head injuries.

'I would like Professor P.N. Tandon to go and visit my relative,' she demanded.

'I am sorry but as director, I cannot tell Professor Tandon to visit another hospital. Only the Prime Minister, the health minister or the president of the institute can do so. Moreover, it would be better to bring the patient here to AIIMS as we have all the facilities and expertise to handle such cases here.'

'You never agree to anything I ask,' she shouted.

She continued to harbour some resentment against me when the famous actor Raj Kapoor fell ill in Delhi. He had come to Delhi to receive an award and brought his portable oxygen cylinder with him for his chronic lung disease but developed difficulties. He was brought to AIIMS and admitted to the ICU. We gave his family a private room. When Rajiv Gandhi came to visit him, Mrs Raj Kapoor asked for an extra external telephone line, which we installed. As for myself, I asked Rajiv Gandhi for extra security as the crowd outside the hospital was growing and I was not sure if we could manage. Reinforcements from Haryana police were sent and posted at the hospital entrance.

When a young doctor returned from lunch, the police failed to realize he was a doctor as he was not wearing his white coat or stethoscope, and they blocked his entry with *danda*s. Word spread. Tension rose among the faculty, and residents called for a 'tools-down strike'.

I had to ask for the Haryana police to be removed and for plainclothes policemen to be posted there.

The health minister was not in Delhi, and at a meeting held by the deputy health minister to review the arrangements for Raj Kapoor, she lit straight into me, telling everyone present that Rajiv Gandhi was not happy with my arrangements. This was a false accusation, for I and my team understood that Bollywood stars are heroes to the Indian population and we were looking after security as much as we were nursing Raj Kapoor. When I contradicted her, she lost her composure.

'You always walk around with your nose in the air,' she said and burst into tears.

Dr Safaya and I left the meeting as soon as possible to continue with our work.

Sometimes the presence of a politician in the hospital could create funny moments. The minister of communications was admitted with a minor problem. This was the 1980s, when you had to join long queues if you wanted an external phone connection. On passing his room one day, I was taken aback at the long queue outside his door. Politicians often had many visitors but never to this extent. Back in my room, I asked my secretary about it. I learnt that they were not visitors. They were faculty members standing in line with their application forms for a phone connection.

As the earlier chapters describe, I had built up the radiology department at AIIMS with my team. Stories had amassed about me, such as the time when I walked into the paediatric unit's radiology meeting, took one look at the chest X-ray and said 'wrong film'. Those in the meeting were stunned. I simply pointed out that it was unlikely for an 18-year-old male to have breast shadows. None of them had noticed. I later learnt that I had been dubbed Sherlock Holmes.

As director, though, my task was to build up the entire hospital as an institution, a good place to work and a nursery for future generations of scientists and doctors. The sign on my desk read: Come to me with a problem with at least two possible solutions.

At this point I would like to reiterate the origins of AIIMS as conceived by independent India's first health minister, Rajkumari Amrit Kaur. The Oxford-educated Rajkumari returned to India to throw herself into the freedom struggle and served as Mahatma Gandhi's secretary for 16 years prior to 1947. As health minister, she toured the country to understand what health services Indians needed. One of her big discoveries was that India did not have enough medical colleges and the reason new ones were not being built or existing ones expanded was the lack of teachers. Insufficient medical colleges also meant, of course, insufficient research.

To this end, she piloted the AIIMS bill through Parliament in 1956, endowing it with the mission to pursue education, medical services and research. Thanks to a generous donation by New Zealand, Raj Kumar was able to handpick faculty from home and overseas to join AIIMS.

When introducing the bill in Parliament, Rajkumari stressed one point, 'We are going to start with a medical training centre which will provide undergraduate study to only a very, very limited few. The major emphasis will be on postgraduate study and specialization because one reason for our inability to fulfil the desire of so many states today to have more medical colleges is the lack of teaching personnel. One of the main duties of this medical institute will be to prepare personnel for medical colleges.'

Her hope was that the medical education provided at AIIMS and the influence it would exert, would raise the standards of professional medical training and research throughout India.

In short, she envisioned AIIMS as primarily a *training centre of education and research, not healthcare services.* The reality turned out to be different. The population explosion, lack of resources and poverty ensured that patient care consumed a major part of the time and energy of the clinical faculty. Yet, despite this, AIIMS has managed to excel in research and innovation while also being constantly ranked, year after year, as the best hospital in the country for patient care.

But over time, our teaching standards had taken a knock. Student feedback had told us that not all good doctors and scientists made good teachers. We needed a centre for medical education to train our trainers as it was one pillar of our mission to prepare to meet future medical needs. We only had one room for photography called the 'medical illustration' unit with one photographer. All he ever did was make slides that could be displayed during presentations at conferences or for publications.

I felt strongly that this was a gap that needed filling. I approached the British Council for help and learnt that there was an institute of technology in Dundee, Scotland, devoted to teaching. Dundee University also had a department of medical education in its medical school. Both were competitors. I chose the Dundee Institute of Technology for collaboration in education, but before we could begin, we had to buy the necessary technology (for making slides, for displaying information, for recording how a doctor examined a patient, photography, etc.), and for this I approached the New Zealand

The department staff with Dr Peter Brandt, cardiac radiologist from New Zealand. I am in the centre of the second row.

Embassy with whom we had an ongoing relationship. The New Zealand government agreed to provide us with the technology, leaving me with the task of creating the necessary space for the centre and appointing a chief from our own faculty who could kick start it.

First, we sent senior faculty to Dundee for the summer programme, followed by junior faculty. When they returned, we opened the Centre for Medical Education on the first floor space which had been allocated for the 'History of Medicine', a nice idea but it had never got off the ground. Once we were up and running, we visited the Central Government Medical Colleges of Banaras Hindu University, Aligarh Muslim University and Pondicherry and held workshops on how they could start similar centres.

Biotechnology is technology based on molecular biology, which harnesses cellular and biomolecular processes to develop technologies and products that help improve human health and the health of the nation by the early detection of diseases specific to our country. We collaborated with Dr S. Ramachandran, director of the biotechnology department in the Department of Science and Technology at AIIMS, GOI. It was clear that recent developments in biotechnology dictated that we should expand into this area. We were already running a graduate course in human biology, but the number of students was diminishing. Expanding it to include biotechnology was a good solution as it offered career advancement for students as well as our faculty.

Basic expertise in the area was available in the Department of Pathology. For example, Dr Indira Nath was a very capable pathologist who was working in the field of leprosy. She would be perfect to head the centre of biotechnology. Dr Ramachandran and I pushed to get funds for a building and for upgrading Dr Nath to professorship. We started recruiting faculty to work in the areas of tuberculosis from the biotechnology aspect.

Thus was born the Centre of Biotechnology, which grew to acquire a national and international status. The Centre added to the advancement of our research vertically and horizontally. Its notable contributions have been breakthrough research in malaria, TB and cancer biology.

We were running a successful community and public health department. Epidemiology was a part of this team's training but it was not part of clinical practice or teaching. Epidemiology is the science of diseases and how diseases spread to humans. It helps to control and limit the spread of pathogens and other negative health problems. It is a scientific system and data-driven. Epidemiology looks at the distribution and frequency-pattern determinants and the risk factors of health-related states and events. This includes not just diseases and their treatment but also environmental exposure, food-borne illnesses, cancer and birth defects. For policy makers, it is very useful in identifying patterns and the underlying causes.

International Clinical Epidemiology Network (INCLEN) was (and still is) an international network of healthcare professionals (clinical epidemiologists, biostatisticians, health social scientists and other health professionals) who apply multidisciplinary approaches to identify best practices to improve public health. It achieves this by using the network to conduct collaborative, inter-disciplinary research on high-priority health problems, and to train future generations of leaders in healthcare research.

The Network approached the health ministry saying they would be willing to train two physicians in this area, a sunrise subject for clinicians, as it would upgrade our health and medical publications and research. The ministry sent the INCLEN representative to our community medicine professor, Dr L. Nath, for consideration. I told Dr Nath we should not miss this opportunity since, as a clinical radiologist, I had been having interactions with all clinical assistant professors and was aware of their strengths and weaknesses. I chose Dr J.N. Pande from general medicine and Dr Srinath Reddy from cardiology to be sent for training in clinical epidemiology.

The Network sent Dr J.N. Pande to North Carolina in the USA and Dr Srinath Reddy to McGill University in Canada for one year. After returning, both of them proved to be great assets in raising our standards of research and publications. Dr Pande rose to be professor of medicine at AIIMS and established the first medical ICU at AIIMS. He was a top chest physician whose publications on environmental exposure to pollution in Delhi were used by the Supreme Court of India in its recommendation to the government. After retirement from AIIMS, he served as a consultant physician at Sitaram Bhartia Institute of Science and Research. Sadly, he died before his time, at the start of COVID-19 in 2020. He was presented the Padma Shri Award posthumously.

Dr Srinath Reddy became professor of cardiology at AIIMS. After retiring, he laid the foundation of the Public Health Foundation of India, with branches in many states, and acquired national and international importance in the field of clinical epidemiology and public health. He served as president of the Public Health Foundation of India and, during COVID-19, offered a sane and experienced view, both for experts and the public. He was on many WHO committees dealing with clinical epidemiology. He was also presented the Padma Bhushan Award.

So much of what happened at AIIMS involved politicians eager to interfere and flex their muscles. When choosing individuals like Dr Reddy and Dr Pande, I only used the criterion of excellence and integrity. A politician would have his or her own reasons for promoting someone and could question my choice. Luckily, in this case, I was allowed my choice and the later illustrious careers of both doctors vindicated it and made me proud. In this way, clinical epidemiology was established as an expansion to our teaching and training programmes. It both enhanced our clinical services teaching and raised the standard of our publications and analysis. The pandemic later highlighted the need for expertise in this field.

As a practising physician, my husband told me that there was no expert in the area of haematology in the city of Delhi to whom he could refer his patients. Haematology is the study of blood and blood-forming tissues, including the diagnosis and treatment of blood disorders. I looked through our faculty and found that patients of haematology were referred to a lab in the Department of Pathology that dealt with haematology. On the other hand, paediatric medicine was running a clinical haematology service without expert lab help from the acknowledged lab base. I called Dr Saraya, who was the head of the haematology lab, and Dr Chowdhury from paediatric medicine to form a team, and laid the foundation of a full-fledged Department of Haematology. Patients from paediatrics and adults could obtain detailed and valuable haematology evaluation, and lab colleagues had clinicians to discuss the reports with and follow-up with patients. The Department dealt with both benign and malignant haematology, along with paediatric and adult blood and bone marrow.

AIIMS had a Staff Council for ensuring a peaceful and harmonious atmosphere in the hospital and providing healthy mechanisms for resolving disputes. All heads of departments and a select group of associate and assistant professors – as many as could be accommodated in the boardroom – were members. It was also a forum where I could pass on complaints from the public. Fairly early on in my directorship, at one meeting, I raised what was easily the most common complaint I received from the public – that the emergency department needed to be better run. Our system was that resident doctors from medicine, surgery and orthopaedics were posted and physically present by rotation on the days of their OPDs. Senior staff were on call. If a patient had to be admitted, we had a 70-bed emergency ward. After 24 hours, patients had to be transferred to a department so that the same number of beds were available for emergency patients the next day. All

70 beds were always filled. We did not have a permanent set of beds for those who were admitted via emergency.

The problem was that we had junior doctors in emergency – assistant professors with no professor to oversee them. It was run in an ad hoc fashion without proper protocols or designated hierarchy among the doctors. Not being trained in emergency or trauma medicine, the resident doctors treated patients coming in the way they treated all patients, that is, in a totally unhelpful way.

'I could hardly breathe,' said one patient, a middle-aged man, to me later about his experience of being wheeled into emergency. 'I desperately needed oxygen but instead of giving it to me immediately, the doctor on duty asked me my name, my address and my income. I shouted at him, 'Put down Rs 10 lakh, put down Rs 20 lakh as my income but first give me oxygen!'

He had to drag the oxygen cylinder towards himself and clamp on the face mask because the doctor was so bureaucratic and slow.

After hearing numerous complaints of this kind from the public, at the next meeting of the Staff Council, I decided I would tell everyone that we had to create an emergency department. Emergency medicine is a specialty that focusses on providing immediate care to patients with unexpected illnesses or injuries that require immediate medical attention. General medicine focusses on providing comprehensive ongoing care to patients for chronic conditions, preventive care and routine check-ups. Emergency medicine concentrates on acute care and immediate interventions. Emergency medicine physicians manage the full spectrum of physical disorders. They are experts in identifying the critically ill and injured and providing effective and immediate care.

At that time, emergency medicine was only a distinct department in some American hospitals with dedicated staff but not in India. Later, it became a specialization all over the world. At AIIMS, we had rotating doctors untrained in emergency medicine that demands rapid action and thinking on your feet. One day, an assistant professor in orthopaedics would be posted in emergency who had no clue about the work involved. He or she would know only how to handle fractures, and for a patient gasping to breathe, this was not of much use. On another day, it might be an assistant professor in paediatric medicine. On a given day, two to three doctors would be on duty.

To my utter shock, the members disagreed.

'We are a specialist hospital and cannot take on this responsibility. AIIMS was created as a specialized centre.'

None of them liked the idea of sitting around in emergency. It offered no career path of advancement unlike other areas, where a doctor could do some OPDs and study his or her subject and become a specialist.

'But we are a healthcare organization and all our departments are intended to satisfy the public. It is time now to cater to another need, the need for emergency as a specialist department,' I said.

But the Staff Council remained adamant. Every time we debated it again, there was no shift in their attitude. I found myself in the position of knowing that I needed to create a new emergency department but also knowing I could not do it without the staff's cooperation. I settled for creating the post of assistant professors specifically for emergency as a way of improving our standards of delivery. For the first two advertisements for assistant professor specifically for emergency, we got no response, no doubt because doctors thought there would be no growth for them in emergency.

When we advertised a third time, two young surgeons applied: Dr Jitender Maheshwari, a postgraduate in orthopaedics at AIIMS and Dr Ajay Kriplani, a postgraduate in surgery. I chose them and watched both of them closely to make sure they were present at all times since they were both surgeons and, like all surgeons, itching to wield the scalpel. Dr Maheshwari used his free time in emergency writing a book because he considered emergency medicine as a dead end.

It came as no surprise to me when, after a few months, Dr Maheshwari and Dr Kriplani came to see me and asked if they could attend the ward rounds of their specialty on their off days once a week to remain in touch with their primary specialty. 'Yes, you may but only if one assistant professor is always there to provide cover,' I said.

Dr Maheshwari and Dr Kriplani performed well in the emergency but their hearts were in their speciality, not in emergency medicine. It was perhaps not realistic on my part to expect them to build an emergency department with the passion and commitment that was required; this was neither their forte nor skill base. They were constantly looking for vacancy in their specialty and to be re-absorbed into the main speciality departments. Once I relinquished charge as director, that is exactly what they did. Many years later, they joined the non-government, not-for-profit Sitaram Bhartia Institute of Science and Research as visiting consultants, which, in my post-retirement years, I happened to head as medical director.

To conclude, I failed in my responsibility to build an emergency department at that time. Twenty years later, I was invited to inaugurate the Department of Emergency Medicine and did so with great pleasure. Later still, the MCI created a degree in emergency medicine in addition to family medicine, as did the National Board of Examination.[*]

By this time, AIIMS was not a single hospital but a complex of facilities. In 2023, it catered to about 1.5 million outpatients and 80,000 inpatients, and performed over 100,000 operations per year. Among the areas pioneered by AIIMS are cardiac catheterization, heart valve surgery, portocaval surgery, neonatal surgery, joint replacement, cochlear implant and multiple organ transplants (cornea, kidney, bone marrow, heart and liver).

As for technology, AIIMS offers the latest. My successors functioned like me, in that whenever we heard of a new advance or a new piece of equipment, someone somewhere in the Institute took the initiative and mustered the energy and drive required to get it. Just as I was conscious of the need to train physicians and surgeons who could spread out across India, other directors too have built on this. Over decades, a large proportion of neurologists, neurosurgeons, cardiac surgeons, paediatric surgeons and gastroenterologists who started their careers at AIIMS – because it was the first to start courses in super specialities – have gone on to serve patients in other cities and towns.

My baby, the radiology department that I had developed from scratch, grew from one faculty member to 16 today in the general department and from one junior resident to 36 today. The divisions of cardiac and neuro cut the umbilical cord from the main department and became independent departments. Intervention radiology remains with the general department, which is now known as the department of radio diagnosis and interventional radiology.

Leadership is a crown of thorns; you have to wear it with humility and grace, but you also have to be prepared to bleed and suffer at times. I am thankful to all – too many to name – who came to my help whenever required. My directorship started with an assassination that convulsed the entire country and plunged it into tumult but ended quietly with a small farewell party, some speeches and the gift of a silver plaque engraved with the words 'With affectionate regards, from a grateful faculty of All India Institute of Medical Sciences', which I cherish.*

When I retired in 1990, the family situation was stable. My father had died in 1974 and my mother continued to live in the same house in Nizamuddin. My husband was busy as usual with his own practice and with work at Sir Ganga Ram Hospital. But by now Sandeep and Anju had grown up. After school, Anju studied German at Jawaharlal Nehru University. I did mention to her that Spanish would be a good option but her friends were all reading German as it was the best-taught language in the School of Languages. Amar and I only suggested options to our children, we never forced anything on them. All we insisted on was that after qualifying, she should be able to stand on her own two feet financially. After graduating, Anju joined a travel company in 1980 where she met her life partner, Sanjay Varma. They married in 1983 and set up their own – Senator Travels – in 1986 and are successfully running it. Sandeep gave me a restless time, though. He decided to take medicine and passed the first medical entrance exam, which is for the armed forces' medical college in Pune. The last medical entrance exam is for AIIMS. In between these two examinations, he came one day to discuss something that was on his mind. I was taken aback when he spoke. 'I don't want to sit the AIIMS entrance exam,' he said.

'But no one forced you to take up medicine,' I replied. 'It was your own choice. What's happened?'

'It was just taken for granted that with both parents being doctors, I should also take up medicine, but I don't want to.'

I was shaken. My main worry was that admission to the best universities in Delhi was over and he might be left with a second or third choice. Our discussion was inconclusive, and my son went back upstairs to his room while I waited anxiously for Amar to come home so that I could consult him. To be honest, I was bewildered.

'Your son wants to speak to you,' I said to my husband as he walked in later, trying not to betray my anxiety. When the three of us sat down, Amar, loving and serene by nature, patted Sandeep's back and asked him for his reasons. Sandeep said there was no particular reason. He simply didn't want to take up medicine as a career. But, I interjected in a slightly shrill voice, the admissions to good universities in Delhi were over so where will he get admission? At this point, Amar turned to me and said calmly, 'Do you want a third-class doctor son or a first class Harvard graduate? Let Sandeep do whatever he wants to do. You cannot force him to take up medicine. Just accept his choice and do not worry. It is going to be his life and we should leave the choice to him.' He sounded so much like my parents that it was uncanny.

The matter was closed and I calmed down. Sandeep enrolled for Bcom. Honours in Delhi University and later started working for TISCO, Tata Iron and Steel Company, in Jamshedpur. After five years, he was posted to Calcutta and subsequently, with two other colleagues, they set up RAWNET Private Limited and started to import for coal and steel making with Tata's as their main clients to start with and now import from all over the world in their own vessels – Naria, Azure and Emerald – to many other steel making companies. He has proved his father right.

10

VIP Tales

At this point in my memoir, having retired from AIIMS, I'd like to make some broader observations based on my time at the hospital such as the VIP culture, which pervades every corner of the Indian society. The VIPs came in all shapes and sizes. Some were smart, elegant and erudite. Others were thugs. It was an occupational hazard of working at AIIMS that we often found ourselves caught in the cross hairs of politicians seeking favours or seeking to throw their weight around as though the hospital was their private backyard. Elaborate protocols had to be followed for Members of Parliament (MPs), ministers, dignitaries or heads of states from South Asia. They expected privileges. No one less than the top specialist in the required field was to attend to them. Some of them expected us to fuss around them as though their presence lent honour to the hospital and this invariably applied more to the lower echelons than to those at the very top.

When Dr K.L. Wig, professor of medicine, was called in to examine Prime Minister Pandit Jawaharlal Nehru in 1962, a few weeks before the Sino-Indian War, he found that he had fever with no localizing signs and that he was hypertensive. In fact, he had been hypertensive for years and had consulted some British physicians but no medication had been prescribed for it. I was working in the radiology department of AIIMS as a junior assistant professor and my boss, Dr Gadekar, was on leave. I was told to organize a chest X-ray, which I did, and after seeing it, I asked for permission to do a barium study to exclude any other abnormality. This was my first exposure to the security protocols surrounding prime ministers. In anticipation, I had prepared the barium suspension to administer to Pandit Nehru if required. I learnt my first lesson on security protocol. His security personnel threw the prepared suspension in the bin immediately. I had to open a new sealed packet of the powder in their presence and prepared the suspension in front of them before it could be administered.

Interestingly, the chest X-ray revealed an aneurysmal dilation of the aorta and no other abnormalities. The heart size was normal and there were no abnormal glands or any tumour. No active intervention was required for this condition. Two years later, in 1964, when Pandit Nehru died from a complication of this condition – a dissection of the aneurysmal aorta because blood had seeped into the flanks – I knew my initial diagnosis had been correct as this is a known complication of cystic medial necrosis of the aorta.

Whenever a dignitary appeared at AIIMS, someone of commensurate seniority was chosen to be part of the team, even though that person might not be the best qualified for the task at hand. When Pandit Nehru arrived a few weeks later for an IVP (an X-ray imaging test that uses a contrast dye to produce images) of the kidneys, Dr Wig told my boss, who was back from his holiday, that the professor of anaesthesia, no less, would administer the required contrast media for the intravenous study. I was very junior at the time but I did plead repeatedly with Dr Gadekar to let me or the senior resident,

Dr Shyam Sharma, administer the contrast injection because we did at least half a dozen of them every day. We knew that Urografin, the contrast agent available at the time, tended to be thick and sticky and could cause counter punctures of the veins and extravasation of contrast in the elderly. Pandit Nehru was 73 at that time.

'The decision about who should administer the contrast lies with the primary physician, Dr Wig, and we have to accept it,' said Dr Gadekar.

Two senior doctors were flown in from Bombay. A doctor from the PM's residence was also present and an emergency tray and oxygen cylinder was ready. When the IVP process started, my fears came true. The pale Kashmiri skin of Pandit Nehru looked blue, purple and angry when the expected counter punctures of the veins with extravasation of contrast occurred. It was not a pretty sight. I was waiting impatiently outside the door, looking through the glass at what was happening inside and itching to go in to do the job properly, but without permission, I could not enter. After multiple punctures, some contrast did finally go in and we were just able to visualize the outlines of normal sized kidneys on both sides. A normal empty bladder was also outlined, so a renal cause for the hypertension was excluded.

Fortunately, given the crowd and mass media waiting outside the hospital when he left, Pandit Nehru was wearing a full sleeved kurta that covered his bruised and blotchy forearm, and no questions were asked. Later, in his memoir, *Memories of a Medical Man*, Dr Wig acknowledged his mistake, saying 'I chose the wrong person for this procedure, though many good ones were available.'

Dealing with presidents came with its own panoply of pageantry. Neelam Sanjiva Reddy was appointed President of India in 1977 and Dr J.S. Bajaj, professor of medicine, was appointed as his physician. Mr Reddy was referred to me by Prof Bajaj in 1975 for a barium study of the upper gastrointestinal tract to exclude a duodenal ulcer, a sore in the first part of the small intestine. The chest fluoroscopy done as per my routine protocol before proceeding with a barium study showed normal lung fields. The barium study was normal, and I told him of the negative study.

'Why am I having pain then?' he asked me.

'Sir, that is between you and your physician, I cannot tell you. I was asked to exclude a duodenal ulcer and my study shows that there is no ulcer. Your physician should look for other causes,' I said.

Mr Reddy left, I resumed my other duties and forgot about this conversation.

When he returned to AIIMS two years later for a baseline health checkup as President – part of the standard protocol whenever a new president is appointed – he asked, 'Is the lady who did my barium meal still here?'

On being told that I was, he said, 'All right, I will have her do the tests and come on the day that is convenient for her.'

I fixed Saturday afternoon for his study. The president arrived on time and the chest X-ray was done. On going into the dark room to assess the film, to my horror, a 1 cm nodule was present in the left lung upper, which certainly required further evaluation. Since other tests had been fixed, I did not want to detain the president but confided in his son who was a doctor that further investigations were required and I fixed the following day for them. The president arrived and the necessary investigations were done. Accompanying him was not only the usual security but also his household staff dressed in their regal long red coats and gold belts.

While we waited for the X-ray films to develop in the dark room, the household staff appeared in the President's room carrying an impressively large silver platter on which were placed a silver jug, a glass and a box of 555 cigarettes. On asking his son he said he had been smoking 40 cigarettes a day for the past 40 years according to his son. He had no symptoms from this heavy smoking, but the routine chest X-ray carried out as part of his check-up showed a nodule. Doctors are taught, and I was teaching, that any nodule in the lung of smokers is cancer unless proved otherwise. I was shocked. I did not remember seeing any nodule when I had seen him earlier. But the nodule, combined with the box of cigarettes, prompted me to decide that he must be examined for cancer of the lung, which was later confirmed. Mr Reddy chose to have surgery at the Sloan Kettering Institute in New York and lived for many more years, dying of pneumonia in Bangalore at the age of 83.

Before her assassination, Mrs Gandhi used to come for various investigations with a briefcase full of work. No matter how many times I asked her to turn this way and that way, she never showed any impatience. Once, when she came to visit her aunt Mrs Kaul, she found me there, ready to escort her to Mrs Kaul's room in the morning, and when she returned to the hospital in the evening, I was still on duty.

'What are you still doing here?' she asked me, eyebrows raised. 'I absolutely insist that you go home to your family.'

Having no choice I agreed and left her with the medical superintendent, Dr Safaya, to escort her to the room and back again to her car. As luck would have it, on her way down from the fifth floor, the lift got stuck. Poor Dr Safaya was stuck in the lift with Mrs Gandhi, cursing me. He managed to call a member of staff to solve the problem, but from then on, I resolved that, VIP or no VIP, the lift maintenance people would be present 24x7.

Rajiv Gandhi also came frequently to visit state leaders. But once he came to us directly from the airport because, during a visit to Sri Lanka, an over-enthusiastic Sri Lankan soldier miscalculated during the welcome parade laid for Rajiv Gandhi and hit him with the butt of his gun. The X-rays showed no broken bones or serious injury, and we sent him home with painkillers.

On another occasion, Sonia Gandhi brought a young Rahul to AIIMS after he had been hit with an arrow that grazed his temple while playing with the son of Satish Sharma, a family friend, in a swimming pool. Sonia Gandhi told me that she had to bring Rahul to us because Rajiv was meeting the King of Jordan and the latter had given him a fancy car as a gift, which her husband was keen to drive. We kept Rahul under observation to make sure the eye and ear were all right. Rajiv Gandhi told me that he would come later that evening to cheer Rahul up in the swish new car without any security.

'Mr Prime Minister, you cannot enter my premises driving a car without proper security as dictated in the security protocol, so please let me perform my duty to inform you of the safety protocol, otherwise you will have to dismiss me for not performing my duty,' I told him.

I asked him to come see Rahul but only with the appropriate security. He did not come and we sent Rahul home the next morning.

There were more VIP visits than outsiders might imagine. Thanks to her trust in AIIMS, Mrs Gandhi recommended it to any state politician who needed treatment. Once admitted, she would come to visit them. Leaders from Pakistan and Sri Lanka also came with their retinues. Apart from this, we had to cope with the politicians who had persuaded the health minister, even though this provision did not exist in the Act that created AIIMS, that they should have the right to healthcare at AIIMS. Earlier, all Lok Sabha and Rajya Sabha members had been able to seek treatment at Willingdon Hospital (later called Ram Manohar Lohia Hospital). All 544 Lok Sabha MPs and 245 members of the upper house demanded priority whenever they needed our services and the faculty had to oblige them in addition to their routine work.

Politicians also created other problems. There was an MP whose son was working as faculty at AIIMS and had rented out his flat on the campus to his relatives without seeking permission while going to Russia with his family on a fellowship. The relatives were noisy, made a nuisance of themselves, and staff complained to the security personnel. When it was confirmed that non-AIIMS employees were living in the flat, I asked our security to inform the police and asked them to issue a notice to the relatives to vacate the flat.

The phone rang. It was the MP.

'Mein Institute ki deewaray hila doonga agar aap ne mere rishtaydar ko nikala (I will shake the walls of the Institute if you turn out my relations),' he said to me.

'Sir, the walls of the Institute and my shoulders are not that weak that you can try to shake them. You are on the wrong side of the rules, and as long as I am sitting here, you cannot break the rules and get away with it,' I replied.

We made sure the flat was vacated.

Inevitably, when we were filling vacancies, we got calls from politicians if their relative had applied and failed to be selected. For vacancies, we had a screening committee that excluded those who did not fulfil the requirements. One particular candidate failed to make the grade. A few days later, an MP walked into my room and asked why his son-in-law had not been chosen for an interview. 'I have told him that I will take care of the appointment,' he said. I promised to check the committee's list to make sure that no mistake had been made and said I would let him know.

'But there is no need for you to visit me again. If he is not on the list, I can't do anything about it as we follow the rules strictly,' I said as he rose to leave.

'Dr Bhargava, if my son-in-law is not selected, then your life and that of Dr Venugopal will be in danger,' he said as he walked out of the door.

Deeply upset, I asked security to post a guard outside Dr Venugopal's residence. The guard was instructed to tail him 24x7 as he had a habit of visiting the hospital at odd hours, even in the early hours of the morning, to check on patients. Knowing his likely reaction, I told Dr Venugopal not to resist and assured him that I would post a guard at my home too because the MP had sounded very sinister indeed.

When I checked the list of final candidates, I found no error in the omission of the son-in-law. The MP did not stop there. He must have gone to the health minister to get his way because I was asked by the health minister's personal assistant to put the son-in-law on the interview list. She gave me this instruction in writing. He was added to the list and called for an interview, but the selection committee did not choose him. I continued the guards at mine and Dr Venugopal's homes until one day I heard that the son-in-law had been appointed at Safdarjung Hospital. I breathed a little easier and cancelled our guards.

The attempts by politicians to interfere with the autonomy that the Act of Parliament had given us were unceasing. One night at 11.30 p.m., a visitor came to my residence to register a complaint about the security guard outside the ICU preventing him from entering. He was fuming.

'Dismiss the guard at once.'

'Please have a glass of water and sit down. The guard was merely following rules.'

'Madam, are you blind? Can't you see from my clothes that I am a neta?'

After more of this inane exchange, I called the security officer and asked him to escort the politician to the exit while also giving him the number of the doctor on duty in ICU so that he could check on his relative's condition.

He refused to leave. I invoked the autonomy of AIIMS. His response was to speak to someone on the phone from my house and then turn to me to say that the health minister had ordered the ICU guard's dismissal.

'I have done many favours for many of your doctors and I expect to be allowed entrance whenever I wish.'

I motioned to the security officer who was waiting at the door to take the man away. Struggling and choking with indignation, he was removed from my home at midnight.

Such incidences were frequent and very annoying but I could deal with most of them. However, this interference did not end at the level of petty politicians but went higher up. One health minister called me to his office in Parliament and gave me a list of candidates who should be selected in the forthcoming interviews for vacancies. My instinctive reaction was to rip up the page he gave me but I next decided to keep it as evidence as an example of the political interference that I had to deal with.

On another occasion, the health secretary and director general of Health Services arrived at AIIMS uninvited and, without any preamble, told me they had come to help me select a new dean. I almost fell off my chair and told them I was capable of doing so myself. It was my prerogative as director, but clearly the health minister wanted to control who was chosen as dean. However, I told them, 'Since you have come, I can show you the list of the faculty by seniority, but you have to leave the choice to me.'

They looked at the list and said they wanted the candidate who was twenty-seventh on the list in terms of seniority. I told them I will resign. I cannot do this.

'It's the minister's wish,' they said.

The director general prepared minutes of the meeting held between the three of us and named the dean of their choice. I put down my dissent, they signed the minutes and took them for the minister's approval. The director has the responsibility to appoint the dean considering seniority and suitability and it has to be approved by the Health Minister.

I was so upset that evening that I could not sleep, worrying about how to handle the situation. Early next morning, I got a call from the joint secretary who was responsible for interaction with AIIMS, who told me that the minister had been moved to another portfolio. I asked the joint secretary to send the minutes back to me. I told him that I would send a letter to the new health minster informing him that I would be appointing the most senior professor on the list who was capable and suitable but who I knew was not keen to take on the responsibility. I appointed a capable assistant professor as sub-dean to assist him and thus averted a crisis. This was divine intervention, and justice was done.

These shenanigans went on inside the rooms of AIIMS, away from the wards and OPDs. I had to constantly keep reminding myself that my duty was to patients above all else, and no politician or VIP could be allowed to interfere in what was the sacred trust that patients placed in us doctors.

11

Life Is Like Riding a Bicycle. To Keep Your Balance, You Must Keep Moving

The chapter title comes from Albert Einstein and applies to my post-retirement years. Except that I did not retire. For the next 30 years, I worked part-time at two hospitals: Sitaram Bhartia Institute of Research and Science and Dharamshila Cancer Hospital. After retiring from AIIMS, I was not ready to start tending the garden or baking bread. All my friends, on reaching 60, not only retired but seemed to think that life itself was at an end. When I celebrated my sixtieth birthday with a party, some asked me why I was still holding birthday parties. This attitude was not for me. I was 60, healthy, active and expert at juggling home and work. My husband was busy as emeritus consultant at Sir Ganga Ram Hospital. Both our children were absorbed in their professions and living independently. My son Sandeep had also got married to a young woman, Monica Khosla, an architect from Calcutta. My mother were nearby in Delhi with stable health, and my siblings were settled in Madras, Calcutta, the USA, Chandigarh and Delhi. My husband and I had friends and an active social life and financial stability.

Even later in my life, when I reached my late seventies and eighties, I never thought of retiring. On a trip to Bangalore once to see the Narayana Hrudayalaya hospital set up by the cardiac surgeon Dr Devi Shetty, I saw a framed photograph of Mother Teresa and thought, 'If a foreigner can keep working in India till an advanced age, why should I ever stop?'

When I was invited to join Sitaram Bhartia in 1991 – 'The radiologist's chair is waiting for you,' said Dr Gopinath – I accepted happily. Many of my dear colleagues and friends from AIIMS had retired and joined Sitaram Bhartia, set amid a leafy forest in Qutab Institutional Area. The building was attractive and my old colleagues were there, but I knew there was not enough work for me. Nonetheless, I joined in the expectation that the volume of work would grow.

I went to work there three days a week. In an emergency, the films could be sent home for me to examine. The first issue I tackled was the most basic. In developed countries, according to WHO, as many as 1 in 10 patients are harmed while receiving hospital care. The harm can be caused by a range of errors or adverse events, and it can safely be assumed that the figure must be higher in our country. At any given moment, 1.4 million people worldwide suffer from infections acquired in hospitals. Hand hygiene is the most essential and cheapest measure for reducing hospital-associated infection, which is why I badgered the nursing staff constantly and put systems in place to reduce the chances of infection.

I asked for an ultrasound machine to be purchased. An emergency room was created. Owing to the famous doctors at the hospital, it appealed to patients looking for eminent personages to treat them. Word of the hospital spread by word-of-mouth. The Bhartia business family, in particular Abhishek Bhartia, who started the hospital, saw it not as a business but as a noble mission to provide good patient care. I had received a few offers from individual practices in the private sector but the non-commercial character of Sitaram Bhartia appealed to me.

I was not getting any intellectual or academic stimulus from the small amount of work in the radiology department, but it was difficult for the founders to find a good full-time radiologist for a small hospital because technology had grown so fast that radiologists who wanted to remain at the forefront wanted to be able to use the CT and MRI machines, which the hospital could not afford at the early stages. This lack of equipment was why we had no cardiac surgery or neurosurgery. It remained, therefore, at the level of a secondary-care general hospital, albeit with a wide range of specialties. Doctors were not given any 'targets', and no unnecessary tests were to be carried out.

Many years later, when I was 78 years old, I was asked to become the hospital's medical director, which I accepted readily as there was not enough work in the radiology department to keep me fully occupied. In taking over responsibility for the functioning of the hospital, I realized it lacked proper systems and accountability. In order to understand what was needed, I began taking a physical round of the hospital every day and visiting patients in their rooms.

Nurses were not prompt to respond – this was the biggest complaint. We had a rapid turnover of nursing superintendents because they were not able to teach the nurses or empower them. I recruited a nursing teacher who would exclusively train the nurses in the delivery of their services by introducing themselves to the patient when they come on duty and telling them that they would respond to every call bell and never let them go to the washroom on their own because that is when most falls occurred. We drew up a regular nursing teaching schedule. On my rounds, I encouraged the nurses to make friends with patients and strike up a rapport. I wanted them to be so familiar with their patients that on my rounds, they had the answers to my questions on the tips of their fingers. Every day, I hammered home, to the point of tedium, the need for patient safety, infection control and quality care.

The equipment maintenance staff had to be trained. It was well known that at least 50 per cent of medical equipment in developing countries is unusable or partly usable due to lack of skills or parts. This could lead to substandard or hazardous diagnosis or treatment and pose a threat to patient safety. Industries with a perceived higher risk, such as aviation and nuclear plants, have a much better safety record than healthcare. For example, there is one in a million chance of a passenger suffering harm while in an aircraft while there is a one in 10 chance of a patient being harmed while receiving healthcare.

On my rounds, I inspected the labour room, the operation theatre and the kitchen. I rammed home the need for perfect sterilization systems of equipment and laundry and the proper discarding of used needles and syringes. Each year, unsafe injections cause 1.3 million deaths and the transmission of blood-borne pathogens such as hepatitis B and HIV. Hospitals could not be too strict.

Gradually the situation improved as the various managers realized that I was following up and wanted details of progress. But I acquired a reputation for strictness which has the potential to be counterproductive. I tried to soften my image by organizing monthly birthday parties for staff and celebrating International Nurses Day on 12 May. It is a hard balance to strike: demanding high standards but without making staff hostile or affecting their enjoyment of their work.

When we applied for accreditation of the hospital by the National Accreditation Board for Hospitals and Healthcare Providers, officials from the Board spent two days at the hospital and their verdict was: 'Dr Bhargava, you run this hospital like a bullet train.' Of course, they found some areas of non-compliance, which we were obliged to address within a specific period but we ultimately earned the accreditation. We have kept up the accreditation and have consistently improved our standards.

As medical director, I had to deal with every facet of the operation, from the security guards to middle-level managers to senior surgeons and the senior dignitaries who came to us for treatment, such as judges, governors of states and Delhi Chief Minister Sheila Dikshit. No matter how rich or powerful our patients, they almost always asked for discounts. To back their demand, they sometimes cited minor deficiencies or questioned the ethics of the hospital, which used to infuriate me. If any mistake occurred in the billing, I would instantly get it rectified.

We created a blood storage centre and an infertility centre. We also conducted research that was noted by government bodies such as Niti Aayog and the Ministry of Health and Family Welfare, especially the contributions that focussed on the underprivileged. We started a tradition of continuous

The Woman Who Ran AIIMS

education in-house by inviting experts so that we were all abreast of the latest developments, and later – when the patient numbers could justify the investment – we bought our own CT scanner.

The work was tiring but I loved it. I never understood why my friends, who had retired on turning 60, kept asking me, 'Sneh, why are you doing all this? Why don't you take it easy instead?' When they met my mother, they would ask, 'Why don't you tell her to stop?' Her reply would be: 'If she's happy working, why should I stop her?'

I liked my structured day – getting up at 6 or 7 a.m., having a cup of tea and a chat with my husband, doing yoga that I had started when I was young and continued throughout my life, getting dressed and calling the driver to take me to Sitaram Bhartia or to Dharamshila. My life was regulated and it worked for me. On coming home, usually before my husband who used to go to his clinic in the evening when he had finished work at Ganga Ram, I would do some gardening. When he came home, we shared a drink – beer for him, wine or shandy for me – and then dinner. This was pretty much our daily routine, though we avoided junk food and smoking. When we first married, Amar used to smoke. 'Physician, look after thy lungs,' I said to him. After that, he gave it up. Throughout my seventies and eighties, I was on no medication, though I took a calcium supplement for my bones. In my late seventies, I developed hypertension, but I was free of all other ailments.

At weekends, we met my parents or my husband's relatives would sometimes come to stay. We followed this routine for nine years after I retired as director of AIIMS in 1990. My husband died while still working, suffering cardiac arrhythmia in 1999 at the age of 77. We had been married 40 years. After his death, I saw absolutely no reason to stop working at Sitaram Bhartia. If anything, the motivation was even stronger. Why stay at home all day feeling sad and melancholic when I could be helping patients amid all the hustle and bustle of a busy hospital? If I am fit and healthy, I must be out doing something useful. I was not consciously following any plan at all but studies have since shown that social interaction, having friends, a happy home life and a sense of purpose are vital for a healthy old age. I have tended to live by the principle that 'Enthusiasm is the baking powder of life. Without it, you are flat. With it, you rise.' In addition, I never stopped learning. Even in my nineties, I continued to attend the weekly Continuing Medical Education meetings at Sitaram Bhartia.

After my husband's death, I kept up all my social activities – meeting friends, attending the regular kitty party every month and participating in the New Friends Colony neighbourhood group. Working and remaining on the move kept me fit and energized. My mother, who was in her late seventies, moved in with me for a year after his death to provide moral support, but then I continued my life as it had been with him. I missed his companionship and support but work had to go on. As the decades rolled along, it was amusing to find that not only were all my contemporaries long retired (and some were passing over to the other side) but even some of my students, much younger than I, were retired. For me, a good life is one where there is always something to do. I have never been bored, not for a single day.

In fact, if it had not been for COVID-19 when the government urged senior citizens to remain at home, I would have continued at Sitaram Bhartia. Even at 90, I had no medical problems. Aging has not been a painful process for me, except, of course, losing relatives and friends. This, too, I have accepted philosophically. We all have to go one day and they have just gone a little earlier.

With everything running smoothly at Sitaram Bhartia, Abhishek Bhartia, owner and director, asked me to continue indefinitely as medical director, which I did. After 30 years at AIIMS, my total tenure at Sitaram Bhartia lasted 30 years until the last National Accreditation Board for Hospitals and Healthcare Providers's inspection during the pandemic – carried out virtually – and I am very grateful to the Bhartias for the opportunity they gave me to serve society until the age of 90.

In 1990, towards the end of my directorship at AIIMS, I ran into a woman in the corridor who stopped me in my tracks to introduce herself as Dr Suvarsha Khanna, a fellow alumnus of Lady Hardinge Medical College.

'My father was diagnosed with stage IV cancer in 1981 and I realized there was no comprehensive cancer care facility, not only in Delhi but also in the whole of north India. People are forced to go to Tata Memorial Centre, Bombay. My father could have been saved if there had been early detection systems in Delhi. But he died. I am passionate about setting up a dedicated cancer hospital aimed at early detection, improving cures and decreasing death rates. However, I am a paediatrician and I have no knowledge, experience, skills or money,' she said.

'What about the Institute Rotary Cancer Hospital at AIIMS?' I asked.

'It's a start,' she said. 'But it only has 25 beds. When you retire from AIIMS, can you please help me build a cancer hospital? I have registered an NGO, the Dharamshila Cancer Foundation and Research Centre, in memory of my father Dharam Saran Khanna and have been allotted two acres of land by the Delhi government in Vasundhara Enclave, in southeast Delhi.'

She was, of course, right. In the early 1990s, there was no hospital in Delhi or north India providing exclusive cancer care under one roof. Tata Memorial in Bombay was far away and overcrowded. The second option was the Medical College in Lucknow. Travelling to distant places placed families under great stress and deprived them of the emotional support of relatives and friends in their hometown. Distance, or the travel burden, is known to have a negative impact on cancer patients.

In developed countries, almost all the studies demonstrate that patients who lived far from hospitals and had to travel, had a more advanced stage at diagnosis, lower adherence to encoded treatments, a worse prognosis and a worse quality of life. A diagnosis at an earlier stage can allow for less-invasive, more efficacious and less costly management. The time costs associated with travel are an important component of the full economic burden of cancer. Imagine for a moment how much worse this situation is for underprivileged Indians who cannot even begin to think of travel costs, of finding somewhere to stay (there is a limit to how long they can live with relatives) and of food costs, all on top of the treatment costs.

Distance, even in the West, can influence the choice of appropriate treatment by cancer patients. Some studies have found that breast cancer patients living farther from a radiation treatment facility more often underwent mastectomy instead.

Distance also means a worse prognosis for patients because living a long way from the hospital makes it harder for them to comply with the treatment and follow up.

Dr Khanna's idea was magnificent, and I was so impressed by her resolve and passion that I spontaneously agreed to help her in any way I could. She was going to be starting from scratch, literally, and I had three decades of academic and administrative experience. At the time I met her, I was not able to help as I was still at AIIMS. Even post retirement, I was already working three days a week at Sitaram Bhartia. Nonetheless, I decided I could devote three days to Dr Khanna's project. I, too, was acutely aware of the lack of cancer facilities in Delhi and the north and felt it was important to provide such a service as the need was great.

At the moment of saying 'yes', I had no idea that reaching the plot required crossing the Yamuna via boat bridge and various overflow channels – drains – that belonged to the irrigation department and a rough patch of road belonging to the Uttar Pradesh government. Dr Khanna soon realized that getting the allotment of land was the easiest part of the whole venture. Every single step of the way otherwise required dealing with multiple departments of the government and masses of red tape. Dr Khanna took on this exhausting and onerous task. She had to run around endlessly and cope with corruption at every step of the way. It took her no less than two years to receive permission to build.

She selected an architect, but he had no idea about hospitals, nor about the atomic energy regulatory rules on radiation protection and the disposal of radioactive fluid.

Even after we had managed to get a proper road made to reach the hospital, the *nallah* (drain), which ran parallel to the plot, remained uncovered. Side by side with running after permissions, Dr Khanna displayed immense courage, skill and passion in raising the funds she needed. She put in her own money too, and her family also contributed, but obviously this was no more than a drop in the ocean. She trained her sights on public trusts, NGOs, philanthropists and industrialists.

We set up a committee of surgeons, anaesthesiologists, radiation oncologists, physicists, pathologists, medical oncologists and diagnostic radiologists to guide the architect in his planning. The committee informed him of the size of the departments needed for each speciality based on patient needs. The result was an exceptionally well-designed cancer hospital. For radiation, we had experts from AIIMS and from Tata Memorial coming to explain the correct building requirements for radiation treatment machines and diagnostic machines, along with the plumbing requirements for the disposal of radioactive materials based on the Atomic Energy Regulatory Board's guidelines.

Eventually, thanks to her grit and hard work, construction of the 300-bed hospital started. Dr Khanna was in touch with me throughout for guidance. She was lucky to find an honest, hardworking and devoted general manager in Mrs Parijata, an MBA graduate with lots of initiative who never shrank from any task. When, simultaneously, it was time to hire consultants and residents, I chaired the selection committee to assess their competence. We selected highly qualified, trained and skilled consultants to help us start the departments. For this – since we were not specialists in all disciplines – we on the committee hired external experts to help us select the specialized department heads who then went on to play a pivotal role in selecting junior staff, residents,

Building Dharamshila Cancer Hospital from scratch

nurses, technologists and support staff. We were ready with the manpower and equipment and all set to start clinical services.

In 1994, four years later, the Dharamshila hospital building was completed and basic equipment acquired, and the hospital started functioning with the OPD and 100 beds. The hospital now had 300 beds and is the largest cancer hospital in north India. People such as Shiela Dikshit, the lieutenant governor of Delhi and President Abdul Kalam – who inaugurated our updated therapy machine, the first in Delhi – were kind enough to spread the word and make the hospital known and visible.

For hospital equipment, we formed a purchase committee with experts and shortlisted vendors. I had a finger in every single pie because I was determined to buy state-of-the-art diagnostic and radiation treatment equipment that would establish us as pioneers, but I was going to drive a hard bargain, and in this, my extensive experience at AIIMS over three decades proved handy in negotiating annual maintenance contracts, terms and conditions, and, of course, the best price. At times, I was able to buy the equipment I wanted for almost 50 per cent of the original quoted price. In fact, most vendors of hospital equipment knew me and were resigned to my accepting only the best price and not tolerating anything but the minimum equipment downtime.

One of our tasks was to devise comprehensive treatment plans of international standards depending on the type of tumour, its size, stage and presence of other comorbidities. This tumour evaluation ultimately enhanced the outcomes. A daily meeting was set up at 4 p.m. with me as chair so that all clinical consultants could meet with staff from radiology and pathology to get their inputs. This kind of teamwork was of great benefit to patients since it meant that nothing was missed and that everyone was on board and well-informed about the disease.

We approached the National Board of Examination to start a diploma in oncology, which did not yet exist. The idea was for residents to be able to look forward to careers in oncology and encourage the emergence of clinical experts and researchers. We fulfilled the Board's requirements and, in a ground-breaking achievement, the Board gave us accreditation to start a programme in medical and surgical oncology. Dharamshila became the first cancer hospital in India to be given such accreditation.

We became the second hospital in India (after Tata Memorial) to start a post basic diploma in nursing oncology in 2010. It was a tough job for a small hospital but it was needed for the specific care that cancer patients needed. An oncology nurse reviews the treatment plan with the oncologist, is aware of expected outcomes and possible complications, and independently assesses the patient's general physical and emotional status. Oncology nurses have a huge set of responsibilities. Nursing care plans for cancer involve assessment, support for chemotherapy and radiation, pain control, promoting nutrition and providing emotional support. We also started a training programme for technicians specializing in the operation theatre, radiology and pathology.

My first love and responsibility was to set up an excellent department of radiology. We started with a Siemens imported X-ray machine for general radiology, an X-ray mobile unit for the wards, an ultrasound machine and a CT scanner, but I soon realized that we needed a mammography unit. However, with limited funds, this had to wait. A friend of mine, Kamla Kapahi, Austrian by birth, learnt that I had joined Dharamshila and, being a philanthropist, donated a mammography machine, the best of its kind at that time, at a cost of Rs 25 lakhs.

In 2012 we became the first hospital in Delhi to install a high-definition PET-CT. We were now updated in all imaging modalities. In 2014, we bought an MRI machine. We all know the revolution the MRI has wrought in medicine. It made it possible to non-invasively image soft tissues like the brain, heart and muscles. There are about 4,500 MRI scanners in India today, about a third of the number required, given the population (Japan has the highest density of MRI units, with 57 available for every million of its population). The high cost of the machine is prohibitive. But with GDP growth at around 7 per cent per annum, we may be able to acquire MRI equipment more easily and ensure that its benefits become available even to the poorest in the land.

One obvious area was the consumption of tobacco, for which a de-addiction clinic was started. In our country it was not cigarettes but beedi smoking, hookah and chewing tobacco that were the main culprits. The most common was chewing tobacco, which causes cancers of the oral cavity. These malignant lumps and bumps did not require medical therapies or radiation to be controlled but required to be prevented by awareness and advice.

When a senior radiotherapist, who had been trained in England and returned after five years, told me that the lumps and bumps caused by cancer were not decreasing, I started a de-addiction clinic by appealing to consultants to refer their cases and the relatives who came with the patients to the hospital to attend the clinic. It was low cost. We needed no equipment, just a desire to prevent cancer. I urged our radiographer technician to visit the surrounding villages to advise the *pradhan* to hold meetings to discuss the dangers of their hookah gatherings and to attend the clinic. I also gave talks on the dangers of tobacco to the children of the upcoming schools in Vasundhara Enclave because our research and other data showed us that these habits start in the mid-teens from peer pressure. Women were not immune. Though they avoided smoking in public for fear of social censure, they chewed tobacco. Given their subordinate status in families, most of them presented in the advanced stage.

We had joined the Indian Council of Medical Research (ICMR) cancer registry. The council was gathering cancer data from urban India and learnt of the rising rates of breast cancer in Delhi. Acquiring the mammography machine enabled us to start preventive services as well as screening services for early detection, free of charge, otherwise no one would come to us for preventive screening owing to ignorance. We do not have a national screening programme and were not likely to do so, in the near future unlike other countries. We decided to start a local screening programme once I learnt that breast cancer occurred a decade earlier in India than in other countries. It was unlikely that women would come forward voluntarily and pay for screening if they had no symptoms. We started a free screening programme and advertised it. We taught women monthly breast self-examination.

Solid oncology was being handled efficiently and effectively and international standards were being maintained. Solid oncology is the study of solid tumours, which are abnormal masses of tissue that form in organs or tissues and spread to other parts of the body.

While solid oncology was doing well, Dr Khanna was very keen to start a bone marrow transplant unit and liquid oncology. She travelled around the country and abroad to explore and set up the service. Space was available. A strict environmental setup of the building had to be met. Competent, qualified and trained manpower was required. We were lucky to get dedicated and qualified consultants Dr Suparno Chakrabarti and Dr Sarita Jaiswal from Calcutta to set up the bone-marrow transplant unit to international standards.

The success of Dharamshila was a source of great satisfaction to all of us who worked on it alongside Dr Khanna. She brought treatment for cancer to the doorsteps of those living in Delhi and the surrounding region, alleviating much misery and trauma. Distance remains an issue for many patients, unfortunately. Doctors have sought solutions to this problem with telemedicine, which also greatly interested me. Using telemedicine facilities, rural patients can have immediate access to specialist services without having to travel long distances. Chemotherapy can also be supervised with the use of this technology using videoconferencing, allowing patients to avoid long drives or flights. It's possible, of course, that in telemedicine, there is potential for missed information, leading to errors, but this aspect needs further study.

Beyond cancer, in a country like ours, telemedicine can go a long way in providing affordable and quality healthcare to each and every person. It makes the physical location of the care provider and receiver immaterial, reduces the isolation felt by populations who are unable to get quality care due to an inability to travel, provides a platform for training and continuing education of involved personnel without the requirement of travel by either party and reduces the cost of fulfilling the healthcare needs of rural Indians. I believe that since we cannot build a Dharamshila in every town, telemedicine offers a way forward both for serious diseases and for primary healthcare.

In my retirement years, I also served as a trustee for the Kamla Nehru Trust along with Justice Ravi D. Dhawan, a former chief justice of the Patna High Court, and the industrialist R.P. Goenka. The trust ran a district hospital in Allahabad, Uttar Pradesh, and I helped to upgrade the facilities, select the faculty and have it recognized by the University of Allahabad to run postgraduate courses by the university under the National Board of Examinations. We bought radiotherapy equipment for cancer and established an updated radiology department so that the hospital could serve as a cancer care centre for the whole of Uttar Pradesh.

After 30 years of working with the inspiring Dr Khanna, she was kind enough to pay this tribute, 'I have no words to express my heartfelt thanks and gratitude for Dr Bhargava's role as my teacher, guide and philosopher, for shaping my life and empowering me to serve society through the hospital. I wish her a long, healthy and productive life.' She offered me the directorship of the hospital, but it was her baby and I wanted it to remain so and declined.

During this period, large corporate hospitals with deep pockets were making their presence felt in Delhi, and small hospitals could not keep up with the rapidly advancing technology required to remain in the forefront of treatment. Dr Khanna decided, consequently, to look for management consultants and to induct other specialties in order to remain financially viable and, more importantly, to be able to retain manpower. She found suitable management consultants in the Narayana Group of Hospitals headed by the well-known cardiac surgeon Dr Devi Shetty, who was running 27 other hospitals all over the country but who had no hospital in Delhi. After the legal formalities were over, the Dharamshila Cancer Hospital was converted into the Dharamshila Narayana Supespecialty Hospital with new management under Dr Shetty in 2017.

In keeping with its new name, the hospital hired super-specialty consultants and created new departments of nephrology, renal transplant, cardiology and cardiac surgery, gastroenterology medicine and surgery, pulmonary medicine, neurology and neurosurgery and ENT. The management now reported to Dr Shetty's headquarters in Bangalore.

In 2020, when the pandemic burst onto the scene, I was 90 years old and it seemed the perfect moment to hang up my white coat, secure in the knowledge that the hospital that we had worked for was in good hands.

12

All About Doctors

Doctors are notorious for being hypochondriacs. There is a well-documented phenomenon called the medical student syndrome that afflicts students in their first one or two years when they are convinced that they have contracted whatever disease they are studying. They are immersed in descriptions of symptoms without realizing how unlikely they are to manifest themselves. A slight rumble in the stomach becomes appendicitis. A mosquito bite heralds haemorrhagic fever. Everything is cancer. Some are convinced they are going to die of whatever they have tomorrow and rush to emergency where the doctors on duty just laugh at them, calling them a 'cliche'. Of course, they get over this syndrome later.

But my experience has been different. I certainly have never been a hypochondriac despite seeing so many images confirming diseases, and most of the students I have interacted with have also been pretty normal in that regard. Even if they begin as hypochondriacs, as they gain experience, they realize they are not likely to have the disease they are sure they have got. In fact, the opposite happens. They become bad patients, in that they seek medical treatment only when things become dire because they tough it out. Having seen a lot of people who are very sick, they reckon they are probably okay, even if they are not feeling well. Not only do they become inured to pain and sickness in others, they also become tough on themselves and their own complaints.

The COVID-19 pandemic of 2020–21 greatly impacted physician well-being and mental health, with many doctors across the world experiencing feelings of burnout. Not many sought help for their mental health symptoms.

It is also a well-documented fact that suicide is nearly twice as common among physicians compared with the general population. Surgeons are at particularly high risk. A survey in 2021 by the Physicians Foundation in the USA found that more than half (55 per cent) of physicians knew a physician who had considered, attempted or died by suicide in their career. An older survey in 2011 of almost 8,000 surgeons in the USA found that 1 in 16 (6.3 per cent) had considered suicide in the previous year. In my career, I have known personally of two medical students, both male, who died by suicide, unable to cope with the pressure of work.

The pressures of being a resident doctor are hard. At 9 a.m., you start seeing patients in OPD at AIIMS and are meant to continue till noon or 1 o'clock. But you look outside and see a long queue of people still waiting, so there is no chance of going back to the hostel to get lunch, and if you miss the fixed times, lunch will be over. Some doctors, trying to get through the long line, omit the medical history and examination and simply kick the can down the road, that is, they fill out a requisition slip asking the patient to go to the laboratory for blood tests or radiology for an X-ray or an ultrasound. Now the pressure builds up on the laboratory and radiology. How can a radiologist write their report without knowing the medical history and symptoms? It's like working in the dark.

If they make it to lunch, they return and start working with their respective specialist in the latter's clinic in the afternoon. These sessions are vital for them to be able to collect enough medical and case material for their thesis. This goes on till 6 or 7 p.m. Earlier, they used to have two years for their MD, but the pressure to collect sufficient material while doing their other work was immense so we extended it by a year.

Next, rounds of the ward. If, during OPD, patients were admitted, decisions have to be made on starting treatment. If they need surgery, they need a pre-operative assessment to be made. Out of the 20–30 patients the doctor is dealing with on the round, if several need surgery the next morning, it adds up to a lot of work. All the parameters that the anaesthetist will want to know – urine, hypertension, viral markers, haemoglobin levels – have to be arranged. In my time, we had eight operation theatres at AIIMS. Now there are 16. The resident doctor's rounds can last till 10 or 11 p.m. At any moment, there can be a call from the emergency department to attend to a patient. During the week, they also have to make time to attend the Grand Round, which I explained earlier – meetings with consultants of different disciplines to learn from cases. If a patient dies due to uncertain causes and if the family agree to it, a post-mortem has to be carried out and the doctor has to be present. These long shifts are the single biggest cause of stress for doctors. In theory, when the duty list is drawn up in every hospital, the shift is technically for eight hours, but the sheer volume of patients that a doctor has to see, along with attending to patients who are admitted, pushes it routinely into 10, 14, 16 or 18 hours. As one of my colleagues once said,

'One cannot do anything in medicine well on the fly.' This is indisputable. When doctors are seeing over 40 patients a day, they know they are practising substandard medicine.

If India had created good primary and secondary healthcare systems, doctors in hospitals would not be deluged by patients. This has been one of the failures of independent India.

For much of their workday, resident doctors are on their feet. Most hospitals, including AIIMS, have no rest area where you can grab a nap. We have yet to work out a way of combining this level of work with a measure of rest and recuperation. There is no question of being able to take the time to walk back to the hostel, take a nap and return. Impossible. The most you can do is hope to find a chair or stool in the nursing station and take the pressure off your feet there for a few minutes. A social life is out.

This way of living and working is possible only because they are young, their bodies are strong and they are hell bent on becoming doctors. I saw many struggling to cope – no sleep or rest, irregular meals, junk food, no social life, pressure of exams and work. It's a long haul. It begins with five years at medical school. A one-year internship at a hospital, of which six months have to be spent in a village at a primary healthcare centre. Some students love the break this offers them. It's relatively easy. A mother will stroll in with her baby. An elderly man comes for joint pain. A man presents with a cough. You get home nice and early for dinner. The downside is the social isolation and total lack of cafes, cinemas or restaurants.

Then three years of residency begin. Nine years in total. After this, it's a question of choosing a specialization or becoming a general practitioner (GP). It takes 11 years to become a specialist and another 5–10 years before you become a figure that people trust.

It caused me great pain when I used to see doctors becoming qualified and leaving to work abroad. We created the push factors. The USA – or other countries – created the pull factors. 'We have created you. We have spent money on you and kept medical fees low to help you and now you don't want to pay back to society what it has given you?' used to be my reaction.

Over the years, I have seen the number of women going to medical college rising to around half the total or, in some medical colleges, to 60 per cent. I am aware of the low level of women's participation in the Indian workforce in general, and I strongly feel the only way to encourage women to work, apart from creating a safe environment, is for parents to tell them when they very young that they must stand on their own two feet and be financially independent. I have had endless chats with nurses from Kerala and they say they work because their parents dinned it into them that they would have to pay for their wedding and bridal trousseau. Once that was accepted by the whole family, the only question that remained was where to work. Nursing was chosen as hospitals were regarded as safe places. At Sitaram Bhartia, I saw a shift happen that applies to many hospitals – many nurses are now from Manipur. In fact, about 40 per cent of them at Sitaram Bhartia were from Manipur because the Government of Kerala revised their endowments and retained them.

As to medical students, both female and male, I have seen the motivation changing. I used to hear: 'I want to serve my state' or 'I want to serve my country'. Gradually, it became: 'I want to make money. My uncle is a surgeon and he makes a small fortune and I want to be like him.' Surgery, of course, is at the top of the food chain. Every surgeon I have met has been more arrogant than their medical counterpart. Every single one. They are convinced that they are nonpareil.

The word 'vocation' disappeared, and with it, the whole system changed. The fall from grace that doctors have had is partly their own responsibility. They abandoned the earlier spirit that infused medicine – the spirit of a sacred duty to treat patients with empathy and with concern for a human life untainted by any concern with reputation, glory or income.

I know that people think that doctors have to become hardened – or at best dispassionate – to be able to cope with the pain and suffering they see, but that's not strictly true. To be good doctors, they must have empathy and compassion. Empathy is not a frill or extra. Without empathy, the job is mechanical and they are dry, sterile and unpleasant. This does not mean doctors should become emotional with every patient. Becoming emotionally attached turns the patient's problem into their problem. No. But having empathy, putting themselves in the patient's position, feeling for the patient and even feeling emotion to some extent is crucial as it prevents them from making the wrong decisions. But it is alarming how fast doctors' empathy wanes. Studies show that it plunges in the third year of medical school, when initially eager and idealistic students start seeing patients on rotation. It's not that they undergo a Jekyll-and-Hyde transformation. Rather, it is that they quickly become overworked and overtired, and they realize that there is too much work to be done in too little time.

The patient–doctor relationship today is delicate and fraught. How patients feel about their medical interactions really does influence the efficacy of the care they receive, and doctors' emotions about their work in turn influences the quality of the care they provide. Doctors must not lose sight of how patients feel, how they feel the loss of dignity and identity the moment we take their clothes away and lay them in a bed. The only thing distinguishing them from other patients is the particular illness that brought them to us. That is when selfish doctors can extract favours for themselves but not for the profession or the institution which they have promised to serve. I have seen the system becoming more technologically proficient but emotionally deficient. There are cases of missed diagnoses and substandard care that have damaged the trust between doctors and patients.

When money becomes the paramount motive, a system of kickbacks emerge. Someone running a radiology clinic, say, needs patients. I ask doctors to refer their patients to me and in return, I give them a kickback. To finance the kickback and still earn some money myself and also pay for the EMI of the technical equipment I have bought, I have to charge the patient more.

Likewise with GPs and specialists. If I am a specialist in a hospital, I am not operating in the local community. I can either rely on news of my reputation spreading and getting patients by word-of-mouth or I can tie up with GPs to make sure they refer their patients to me. The GPs, who earn very little because they might be located in a neighbourhood or area where people are not well-off, depend on these kickbacks to earn a solid income. They should send patients to specialists only if they cannot handle the ailment themselves, but they refer them to specialists right off the bat. It's mutually beneficial. At Sitaram Bhartia, we decided not to take patients on a referral basis, only by word-of-mouth, for this reason. It took time to get patients. No GP sent us any, knowing he would not get any kickback. When you depend on word-of-mouth patients, it takes time to build up the funds you need to upgrade the equipment and that is the price that has to be paid.

In an ideal world, patients should visit a GP first, not rush to a specialist. A GP conducts a physical examination and has the whole body (maybe even the whole family) in mind when listening to a patient's complaint. If a person complains of backache, the cause may be to do with the spine or it may be to do with the kidneys. The patient does not know. But now in India everyone rushes to a specialist so, having decided their back pain is a spinal problem, the patient goes to a neurosurgeon who is an expert only of the spine and who will start ordering investigations to do with the spine. This leap to a specialist can be disastrous since the neurosurgeon will not even investigate the possibility that the cause of the pain could be elsewhere in the body. The die is cast. The patient might have needed only a few sessions of physiotherapy and some painkillers to feel better. But the patient has entered a tunnel. Perhaps the wrong tunnel.

I used to keep a film of a chest X-ray in the radiology department at AIIMS. It showed a little nodule in the hilar region, the middle of each lung where the bronchi, arteries, veins and nerves enter and exit the lungs. If I showed it to a chest surgeon, he would diagnose a fracture of the rib. If I showed it to a physician, he would say the same nodule was 'a lymph node'. The cardiologist? It's the pulmonary artery. That's why an examination by a GP beforehand is so important. Before homing in on one organ, the whole body has to be considered. By going directly to a specialist, it means that more expensive technology is likely to be used and the costs of healthcare rise.

We have killed the GP in India. It has lost all prestige. There are no high-profile GPs in Delhi. Hardly any medical students opt for general practice or family medicine. It differs from person to person but in our society, a specialist is given more social respect than a bachelor of medicine or MBBS. The intensive training required for specialization can lead to greater professional prestige and esteem within the medical community. Other reasons are, of course, better pay and more professional growth.

Unsurprising, then, that a hospital speciality is the first choice and general practice is a fallback option. Why be a GP who is dependent on kickbacks from specialists to boost what is a low income when you can become a specialist yourself? Why settle for being at the low end of the medical food chain given how much money has been invested in a medical education, money which needs to be recouped? Moreover, how many trainee doctors can raise the crores of rupees they need to buy a GP clinic or pay tens of thousands as rent? How many bright students can pay the capitation fee that private colleges demand for admission to graduate or postgraduate studies?

It is also worth pointing out that healthcare is not only dependent on *medical* care. It is much wider than that. It also depends on clean water, sanitation and effective sewage systems, in addition, of course, to preventive care. If none of these work, people will fall ill. Some of our best brains have failed to grasp this point. Similarly, on population control, the people making the decisions have no idea of the compulsions driving a poor farmer to have five children when the evidence is stark. Since the government has not given him piped water, he needs one child to fetch water. Since no one gave him piped gas, he needs one child to collect firewood. For his cow or goat, he needs a third child to gather fodder. The fourth child is needed to look after the youngest child when the mother goes out to work in the fields. And the fifth child has to be the strongest one to protect the mother when the drunken husband comes home itching to beat her up.

Under the British, we had a system based on a health officer cadre and a medical officer cadre. The former functioned in a district and made sure that the food sold was hygienic and safe, that water was potable and that the drains were clean. The person who looked after illnesses was the civil surgeon. After Independence, we abolished the health officer role, leaving only medical care. It is only recently that we have restored the health service cadre.

In 2022, the government announced it was setting up a central public health cadre for medical professionals along the lines of central services officers recruited through the UPSC. As part of the plan, all health professionals, including those working for the Directorate General of Health Services (DGHS), will be recruited through the permanent cadre and help the government implement healthcare policies. I was very pleased to hear of this decision.

But to come back to doctors and specialization, over the years, the sense of vocation, of serving the community, has given way to simply wanting to make money, and this is responsible for the fall from grace they have experienced. They no longer enjoy the same public esteem. They no longer commit themselves to looking after patients from the cradle to the grave, a concept which in any case has died with the disappearance of the GP who used to know the patient and the patient's family.

As to ayurvedic doctors or any traditional doctor, I have never consulted one for the simple reason that I have no idea what he or she might give me. I do not discount ayurveda. I am sure it has uses, but without research and data from random clinical trials, we cannot establish its efficacy. However, I think the Chinese have got it right. In the fourth year of medical school, students have to learn about traditional Chinese medicine. Their tradition is very strong. Under the British Raj, ayurvedic colleges were banned and important texts destroyed, but in China, the sources of knowledge remained. We, too, need to include ayurveda in the medical curriculum as it is the only way to encourage the research that ayurveda so woefully needs. If you ask ayurveda practitioners today to carry out research of their treatments, they cannot do so as they have no training in research.

As a formerly 'noble' profession, medicine has slipped. I believe the public should treat doctors simply like any other professional – respect their knowledge which they have spent long years acquiring but no extra respect is required for them as individuals. Some doctors have even forgotten to have a good bedside manner. Some do not know how to listen to a patient, which is a critical part of diagnosing and treating. A doctor who is good at listening will pick up multiple little clues, and these are not necessarily what the patient intends for him or her to pick up. Diagnosis is part-science, part-art and much depends on listening and carrying out a physical examination. A good doctor is one who gains the confidence of the patient.

But patients, too, should spare the doctor their own assessment derived from Google and what is often a display of passive-aggression – a tone and manner that suggests they are not necessarily going to believe the doctor or act on what he or she says. And sometimes, naked disrespect. As a random list, doctors are not keen on patients who walk in saying, 'I read on the Internet...'; patients who do not take medication as prescribed or fail to follow the treatment plan; have unrealistic expectations as though doctors can work miracles; families such as those of TB patients who demand a lung transplant; mothers who fail to get their children vaccinated; new mothers when, handed a healthy baby girl, say they wanted a son; alcoholics who have no desire to come off the bottle; patients who turn up so late with a wound that it's infested with maggots; have such low personal hygiene whose feet smell a mile off or who eat stinky food before coming in; call late in the evening to ask inane questions such as pregnant women asking if they can dye their hair; walk in with three pages of questions; stroll in cheerfully texting away and then say their pain is 10 out of 10; bring their child into emergency with a scratch on his face and demand that a plastic surgeon be called in to treat it; or post a scathing online review without giving the doctor an opportunity to resolve the issue.

The most upsetting patient for all doctors is the one whose condition is baffling. Doctors want to cure and are depressed if they are unable to help a patient. Good doctors care about their patients. I knew of top surgeons who, the day before a particularly complicated operation, would visit a mandir to pray for a successful outcome. I knew surgeons who, conscious of the fact that a human life is in their hands, prayed more for the patient's recovery before surgery than the family. For me, that is the definition of care. In my ninety-fifth year, on finishing my memoir, it is my wish that the spirit of public service continues to be the guiding force of the medical profession. As Hippocrates said: 'Wherever the art of medicine is loved, there is also love of humanity.'

Appendix A

My Research and Publications

Besides patient services and teaching, I was also contributing to publishing clinical research in various systems of interest to me. It can be categorized as follows:

a) Contribution to advancement of knowledge in biomedicine across all specialties, with special reference to the imaging sciences, co-relating with clinical assessment.
b) Contributions leading to establishment of imaging departments, and setting patterns of examinations at AIIMS and various parts of the country, with emphasis on quality control and radiation safety in addition to subject expertise had set the standard.
c) Contribution to hospital management.

The contributions made covered a wide spectrum of disorders, with special reference to their image morphology using all imaging techniques in practically every organ system of the body, as evidenced by the list of publications. The contributions spanned a wide field, specifically in:

1. Pulmonary hypertension in rheumatic heart disease
2. TB of the CNS
3. Aortoarteritis
4. Renal hypertension

Pulmonary Hypertension in Rheumatic Heart Disease

Guided by Sir Dr Robert Steiner and Dr Gadekar, I was one of the first to recognize the radiologic pattern of pulmonary hypertension in rheumatic heart disease and grade its severity in terms of hypertension, with an accuracy comparable to cardiac catheterization and manometric pressure studies and measurements.

This work formed part of my thesis submitted to the AIIMS for MD. The pattern and methodology described has stood the test of time and has not yet been improved upon, and now forms the basis of routine diagnostic reporting and teaching for preoperative evaluation.

Along with Dr Gadekar, in 1963, I described the different Röntgen patterns of arterial and venous pulmonary hypertension seen in rheumatic heart disease against the patterns of exclusive arterial pulmonary hypertension seen in congenital heart disease. The key papers here are 3, 6 and 7.

Sir Robert Steiner, professor of radiology, Royal Postgraduate Medical School, Hammersmith Hospital, London, is familiar with this work and offered me a job in his department when he visited our department on a visit to India.

TB of the CNS

Prior to the availability of the CT scan, TB of the CNS was a presumptive and exclusion diagnosis. Exploiting the sensitivity of the CT scan and establishing the CT morphology of intracranial TB as seen in India, both intracranial and spinal.

It has been compared and contrasted to studies done in other parts of the world. Other studies were few in number. My series was one of the earliest reported in international literature, both from the diagnostic and therapeutic point of view. Lessons learnt from this series are also reported. The studies have proved that intracranial TB, hitherto considered a surgical problem, is really a medical problem in most of the cases seen if diagnosed early and can be safely followed on medical management with CT control. This work has totally altered the outlook, management and cost effectiveness of treatment of CNS TB. It has been extensively quoted and now forms basic reference material of this entity. It is one of my most cited papers, not surprisingly. The key papers are 75, 76, 107 and 108.

Professor Torgny Greitz, professor of neuroradiology, Karolinska Institute of Science, Stockholm, and Sir John H. Middlemiss, dean and professor of radiology, Bristol University, are familiar with this work and have seen it on their visits to India. Sir John Middlemiss awarded me the fellowship of the royal colleges of surgeons and physicians of England in radiology.

The CT scan has also been exploited to assess brain damage in tubercular meningitis, an assessment that was only possible at autopsy in earlier years. This study has not only graded the severity of meningeal involvement and brain damage but also established parameters of prognosis and the possible sequelae. It also forms the basis of objective assessment of the associated hydrocephalous and its follow up by medical management or surgical shunting if required.

The key papers are 83 and 102.

Other papers contributing to various aspects of neuroradiology are 1, 5, 14, 20, 22, 23, 50, 58, 60, 71, 72, 100, 106, 111, 113 and 116.

Neurocysticercosis

This parasitic infestation of the CNS is the greatest imposter of all CNS lesions seen by practising physicians in India. Prior to the availability of the CT scan, all suspected patients underwent two or three invasive investigations before even a presumptive diagnosis could be made. The CT scan has been effectively used to establish that contrary to published literature from the West, including Mexico, the Indian disease is of a more acute form seen in 60% of the cases. It excites a cerebral oedema not seen in any other known lesion with episodes that are waxing and waning, and result in 'throttled ventricles', a term coined by me. The Mexican variety leads to hydrocephalous, and the Indian variety leads to cerebral oedema with a graver prognosis if not diagnosed on time.

Recognition of this specific diagnostic pattern has become all the more important now with the availability of praziquintel, a new drug for this condition. Praziquintal itself gives rise to cerebral oedema, and if its therapeutic use is to be utilized its administration should be at a time when cerebral oedema due to the disease is not present, otherwise fatal results would ensue.

Therefore, recognition of the Indian pattern of the disease is vital and has been established by our work. It has opened up the question of proper timing of drug administration. It will form the sheet anchor of diagnosis and management until a more specific serological and immunological test is established. The work was presented at the World Congress of Radiology in Brussels in 1981. The key papers are 78, 86, 98 and 100.

Professor H.W. Pia is familiar with this work. At his request, an article was written for *Neurosurgical Review* in Berlin.

Aortoarteritis

The occurrence of this entity was described in India by P.K. Sen and A.K. Basu in the 1950s, wherein the surgical and imaging aspects were presented. My team and I have worked on the Röntgen and the disease's clinical profile, and have established the Indian pattern as mainly a stenosing arteritis in contrast with the African variety, which is mainly an aneurysmal type.

Because of lymphangiographic studies coupled with histology of the para-arotic nodes, it is now possible to say that associated primary lymph node tubercular disease is coincident and not the cause as postulated by Sen and Basu.

This has led to immunological studies and myocardial biopsy studies. Today, work has been initiated to establish an experimental model for further evaluation of the lymphatic system and the primary target and the ensuing vasculitis as the secondary result.

The key papers are 84–91 and 101.

Renal Hypertension

The profile of renal hypertension in our country has been established by the work done by me and my team and spread over two decades. Parameters of diagnosis have been refined, as new aids for aortography and renal angiography became available.

Aortoarteritis emerged as the single leading cause in 40 per cent of the patients. The establishment of serial arterial studies has helped to separate the primary vascular group from the parenchymal group. These studies have laid the foundation for further work. On the other hand, the long follow-up has provided insight into the prolonged and benign course aortoarteritis takes and, therefore, percutaneous therapeutic measures of renal arterial dilatation have been introduced. Studies are in progress to elucidate this aspect further.

Other works covering a wide front are the following:

Gastrointestinal Radiology: Gastrointestinal Tract

In the early 1960s, when endoscopic evaluation was not available, the main diagnostic brunt had to be borne by radiology and established patterns of advanced carcinoma stomach were well-known but pitfalls in diagnosis not so well-documented, such a study was undertaken and published (6).

Patterns of congenital lesions of the alimentary canal causing obstruction in the neonates and infants have been documented (10). Techniques to carry out these examinations gently and swiftly established and published (39, 84).

Radiological pattern of coeliac disease in North Indian children have also been documented (32).

Double-Contrast Studies

The accuracy of single-contrast gastrointestinal studies in the hands of best radiologists is around 70 per cent. In order to improve on this, Japanese workers perfected the technique of double-contrast gastrointestinal studies. We invited Dr Kobayashi, the Japanese author who developed double-contrast studies of the stomach. Gastric carcinoma is four times more common in Japan than in the UK and occurs at a younger age. However, the basic materials for such studies were not available in the country. Therefore, experiments with various combinations of locally available contrast media and gas-producing agents were initiated and successfully completed for evaluation of the stomach, duodenum and colon by this technique was routinely adopted and correct results obtained was raised to 90 per cent, though we did not publish it – it was my mistake.

Double-contrast study of the oesophagus is an ongoing project at present, the techniques having been established.

Gastrointestinal TB: Neostigmine

Gastrointestinal TB is a common entity in our country, and examination of 6 metres of the gut takes two to four hours. We established that neostigmine-assisted barium meal studies have been carried out bringing the examination time to one hour (49), but the accuracy of diagnosis of strictures caused was usually 50 per cent in the small bowel, but evaluation of the ileocecal junction was 90–100 per cent, which was critical for correct diagnosis.

Studies on the Liver

Radiological evaluation of the liver has occupied my attention for some time. In collaboration with the clinical team deeply interested in the study of portal hypertension, non-cirrhotic portal fibrosis, veno-occlusive disease and obstructive jaundice, techniques of evaluation have been established and radiological patterns of recognition have been documented.

With the availability of ultrasound, studies on the biliary tract and infection-forming abscesses of the liver are documented. The key papers are 62, 104, 109, 115 and 118.

Urogenital System

Up to the early 1960s, the only radiological evaluation of the urinary tract was by intravenous pyelography. In India, evaluation of the renal parenchyma and lower urinary tract was not established andn the evaluation of the lower urinary tract was not done until then. However, these procedures have since been established and their methodologies published. The technique of pelvic pneumography as a diagnostic aid in gynaecological endocrine disorders was first established by me, but not published as the number was too small. With the availability of ultrasound and CT scans, these studies are not required.

Angiography

In renal tumours, it has been analysed in 50 cases and presented at national conferences. Embolization of these has been carried out in some. The key papers are 15–18, 23, 26–34, 39, 41, 89, 109, 112 and 114.

Chest Radiology (Mediastinum)

Röntgen evaluation of the mediastinum has been an abiding interest but not published, except for 1 case – 13.

Osseous Radiology

Patterns of osseous TB have been documented and have stood the test of time. Spinal TB, which forms 52 per cent of osseous TB of bones, has been studied in depth. Patterns have been established documenting primary involvement of bone and separating it from secondary involvement due to soft tissue disease in the tissue planes or surrounding lymph nodes. Publication of osseous radiology covers infections, tumours, bone density, cysts, endocrine disorders, renal failure, unusual osseous deposits, arthropathies and congenital lesions. The key papers are 2, 4, 5, 21, 28, 36, 40, 44, 46, 47 and 50.

Neuroradiology

In the earlier years, contribution to neuroradiology was limited because of the lack of specialized equipment, but over the years, active involvement with neurology and neurosurgical teams and availability of equipment helped to contribute to the neuroradiology literature nationally and internationally. Availability of the CT scanner helped to bring contribution in infectious diseases and of the CNS to the forefront (14, 20, 22, 23, 50, 58).

Cardiovascular Radiology

My earlier studies were on the radiology of pulmonary hypertension. There was no radiological investigation that was not done in radiology with the equipment we had. The clinical disciplines also recognized me to be the leader in developing imaging techniques, as is evidenced by professional societies as diverse as neurology, urology, gastroenterology, paediatric and chest from all over the country. They have invited me as a guest speaker on their important orations and functions. Likewise, apart from medical scientific societies, other allied scientific societies like the Indian Institute of Technology and the Ultrasound Society of the National Physical Laboratory (NPL) have also honoured me and recognized my contribution to imaging.

I was responsible for establishing a fine-training programme for radiologists and radiographers at AIIMS. The training format established has formed the basis of training programmes in many institutions across the country. The emphasis laid on blending clinical history with image morphology and geographic medicine based on community and epidemiologic research of any organ system set the trend for accepting radio diagnosis as a clinical subject rather than para clinical as was the practice.

The change in the concept of the radiologist as a photographer to that of a clinician and a vital member of the patient care team was mainly due to my pioneering efforts. Routine clinico-radiological conferences have been established as a part of the training programme. I was responsible for having introduced new technologies of imaging to the country. The first CT scanner in India was installed at AIIMS under my charge.

The introduction of ultrasound scanners was also largely due to my efforts. Teams of residents and in-service doctors from all over the country came to AIIMS for training in these techniques, mainly because of my efforts in running regular training programmes throughout the year, thus making it possible to extend the availability of this technology to the poor masses and improve healthcare systems. The snowballing effect of high-quality training has been initiated at the national level mainly by my efforts and elevated the standards of medical care.

Interventional Radiology

There was a silent revolution going on in radiology with the introduction of interventional techniques. AIIMS was the first institution in India to establish interventional techniques for both vascular and non-vascular systems, and this was possible because of the efforts that had been put in quality diagnostic set-up, which could take on the responsibility of guided by imaging that would be acceptable to all referring clinicians. The interventional techniques are now well established, teams are available, residents are being trained in this field and necessary manpower is being created to expand and become cost effective all over the country.

Imaging departments are capital-intensive departments, in terms of both initial planned expenditure as well as recurrent expenditure. My contributions have led to the establishment of cost-conscious imaging departments, with radiation safety as the key factor. This is evidenced by the fact that my advice had been sought by practically all national and state institutions in India, including Sree Chitra Tirunal Institute of Medical Sciences and Technology, Thiruvananthapuram; Postgraduate Institute of Medical Education and Research, Chandigarh; College of Medical Sciences, Kathmandu, Nepal; Cancer Research Centre - Jamshedpur; Nizam's Institute of Medical Sciences, Hyderabad; Sanjay Gandhi Institute of Medical Education & Research Centre - Lucknow; Sher-e-Kashmir Institute of Medical Sciences, Srinagar, for the purchase and selection of equipment by their institutions and for training their staff at medical and technical levels.

Quality and Safety

In collaboration with the Southeast Asia region of WHO, seminars on quality control have been organized and published in a book by WHO as a technical series.

Recognizing the continuous efforts of inspiring radiologists and radiographers in quality imaging, WHO assisted me in organizing a national workshop on quality control and assurance in diagnostic radiology. This work is now to be followed by a regional conference on quality control. The paradox is that though a larger part of our population does not have access to diagnostic facilities, those that can avail of them get their share of overdose and poor quality unlike elsewhere in the world.

The emphasis has been on the economic effects of poor-quality radiology to the institution and the extent of unproductive imaging requisitioned by the clinician, over which the radiologists have no control.

The cycle of unproductive imaging is in conflict with the aim of a good-quality, low-dose and cost-effective healthcare system. This has been conclusively proved by my studies on the commonest X-ray examination – the chest X-ray. In an analysis of 2,000 cases, only 30 per cent of asymptomatic patients showed pulmonary parenchymal lesions; 58 per cent of symptomatic patients revealed normal chest X-ray. In the last 10 years, no person among nursing service entrants revealed any abnormality on chest X-rays that was not suspected clinically. Therefore, unproductive imaging could be safely omitted with a cut-down in costs and radiation and increase in good quality. The key paper is 'Health and Economics' in Diagnostic Radiology, the Time Press (1986).

Because of my good track record of establishing and efficiently running a large radiodiagnostic department, the mantle of chair of the Hospital Management Board fell on me in 1980.

For the last many years, this responsibility is being discharged and many improvements are being introduced. A major area was the introduction of the paging system, a long-felt need for effective and quick communication in the hospital when there were no mobile phones.

The reduction in the average length of a patient's stay in hospital by recognizing the role of efficient support systems, so that there is a higher turnover of patients on the same bed strength, has been achieved mainly because of my persistent efforts with the help of post-graduation of the master of health administration (MHA) course.

List of Publications

1962

1. Bhargava S., Bilateral Basal Ganglia Calcification, Ind. Jr. Radio. XVI, 37–40, 1962.
2. Bhargava S., Craniolacunia of the New Born, Ind. Jr. Obst. and Gynae. XII, 497–500, 1962.
3. Bhargava S., Lung Changes in Mitral Stenosis, Ind. Jr. Radiol. XVI, No. 4, 221–38, 1962.
4. Bhargava S., Idiopathic Hypoparathyroidism, Ind. Jr. Neurol. X, No. 147–50, 1962.
5. Bhargava S., Pre-natal Diagnosis of Meningoceles, Ind. Jr. Obst. and Gynae. XII, No. 6, 1962.

1963

6. Bhargava S., Roentgen Evaluation of Pulmonary Hypertension. Thesis submitted to AIIMS as partial fulfillment of MD Radio Diagnosis.

1964

7. Bhargava S., Gadekar N.G., Roentgen Prediction of Pulmonary Venous Pressure in Mitral Stenosis of Rheumatic Origin. A New Approach, Ind. Jr. Med. Sci. 18, No. 5, 259–67, 1964.
8. Bhargava S., Gadekar N.G., Roentgen Diagnosis of Carcinoma Stomach and Pitfalls in Interpretation, Jr. Asso. Phys. Ind. 12, No. 3, 211, 1964.
9. Bhargava S., Bapna B.C., Unusual F.B. in Pelvis, Ind. Jr. Surg. XXVI, No. 4, 519, 1964.
10. Bhargava S., Gadekar N.G., Walia B.N.S., Clinical and Radiologic Diagnosis of Atresia of the Alimentary Tract, Ind. Jr. Radiol. XVIII, No. 4, 165–71, 1964.

1965

11. Goulatia R.K., Bhargava S., Penumatosis Cystoides Intestinalis, Ind. Jr. Radiol. XIX, 1, 41–3, 1965.
12. Bhargava S., Gadekar N.G., Osbil: A New Oral Cholecystographic Contrast Media, Ind. Jr. Radiol. XIX, 4, 204–7, 1965.

1966

13. Dhawan I.K., Kand S., Bhargava S., Germinoma of the Mediastinum. A Case Report, Ind. Jr. Patho. Bacteriol. IX, 1, 97–100, 1966.
14. Virmani V., Bhargava S., Gupta P.C., Gupta S., Penumoencephalographic Study of Atrophic Brain Lesions, Ind. Jr. Neurol. XIV, 1, 19–24, 1966.
15. Bhargava S., Thomas K., Bapna B.C., Gadekar N.G., Obstructive Disorders of Lower Urinary Tract in Infancy and Childhood. 1966.
16. Bapna B.C., Datta N.S., Singh S.M., Chakrabarty A.K., Bhargava S., Bilateral Renal Calculi, Surg. Jr. Delhi. I, 5–10, 1966.
17. Bhargava S., Gadekar N.G., Voiding Cystourethrograms in Paediatric Practice, Paed. Clin. Ind. I, No. 1, 15–19, 1966.
18. Kapoor P., Thomas K., Walia B.N.S., Bapna B.C., Bhargava S., Gahi O.P., Obstructive Uropathies in Children, Ind. Jr. Med. Sci. XX, No. 8, 563–6, 1966.
19. Walia B.N.S., Sidhu J.K., Tandon B.N., Ghai O.P., Bhargava S., Coeliac Disease in North Indian Children, Brit. Med. Jr. 2, 1233–4, 1966.

1967

20. Bhargava S., Mongia S.K., Virmani V., Gadekar N.G., The Pneumoencephalogram in Cerebral Atrophy, Ind. Jr. Radiol. XXI, No. I, 37–47, 1967.

21. Gadekar N.G., Bhargava S., Ghosh S.K., Skiagrams of the Quarter, Ind. Jr. Radiol. XXI, No. 1, 60–3, 1967.
22. Mongia S.K., Bhargava S., Singh B., EEG in Cerebral Atrophy, Ind. Jr. Neurol. XV, No. 4, 179–84, 1967.
23. Bapna B.C., Datta N.S., Singh S.M., Bhargava S., Chawla V., Khandpur S.C., Pheochromocytoma: An Important Cause of Correctable Hypertension (Report of a Case and Review), Ind. Jr. Ped. 34, 410–15, 1967.

1968

24. Devi M.G., Bhargava S., Virmani V., Measurement of Anterior, Posterior and Middle Cerebral Arteries with Special Reference to the Sylvian Triangle in Normal and Abnormal Angiograms, Neurol. Ind. XVI, No. 1, 27–34, 1968.
25. Pathak H., Ahuja M.M.S., Singh S.M., Bhargava S., Gadekar N.G., Rapid Sequence Intravenous Pyelography in Clinically Diagnosed Chronic Pyelonephritis, Ind. Jr. Radiol. XXII, No. 1, 56–65, 1968.
26. Bapna B.C., Chakrabarty S.M., Singh A.K., Bhargava S., Thomas K., Rhabdomyosarcoma of the Prostate, Ind. Jr. Ped. XXV, No. 244, 232–6, 1968.
27. Sikand K.K., Bhargava S., Gadekar N.G., Singh S.M., Roentgen Spectrum Urinary Tract Disorder by Intravenous Pyelography (A Study of 1100 Intravenous Pyelograms), Ind. Jr. Radiol. XXII, 3, 150–6, 1968.
28. Malhotra K.K., Gadekar N.G., Umashankar P., Bhargava S., Bone Disease in Chronic Renal Failure. Ind. Jr. Med. Sci. 56, No. 11, 1687–95, 1968.
29. Malhotra K.K., Ahuja M.M.S., Umashankar P., Veliath A.J., Bhargava S., Clinical and Laboratory Features in Hirsuitism, Ind. Jr. Med. Res. 56, No. 11, 1696–706, 1968.

1969

30. Sikand K.K., Bhargava S., Bapna B.C., Gadekar N.G., The Value of Prone Pyelogram, Ind. Jr. Radiol. XXIII, No. 3, 132–4, 1969.
31. Malhotra S.S., Bhargava S., Pelvic Pneumography: A Valuable Aid in the Study of Hirusuitism, Ind. Jr. Radiol. XIII, No. 3, 143–7, 1969.
32. Bapna B.C., Singh S.M., Chally R., Bhargava S., Ghai O.P., Posterior Urethral Valves: Diagnosis and Management, Ind. Jr. Ped. 36, No. 261, 350–55, 1969.
33. Bapna B.C., Datta N.S., Singh S.M., Bhargava S., Walia B.N.S., Thomas K., Urethral Ectopia, Ind. Jr. Ped. 36, 261, 380–8, 1969.

1970

34. Bhargava S., Bapna B.C., Walia B.N.S., Urethral Ectopia with Incontinence in Female Children, Ind. Jr. Radiol. XXIV, 23–7, 1970.
35. Gupta B.D., Bhargava S., Haldar P.K., Unusual Clinical Presentation of Malignant Renal Tumour (Hypernephroma), Ind. Jr. Radiol. XXIV, No. 2, 134–6, 1970.
36. Dhawan I.K., Bhargava S., Nayak N.C., Gupta R.K., Central Salivary Gland: Tumours of Jaws, 26, No. 1, 211–17, 1970.
37. Chandra R.K., Khanna K.K., Veliath A.J., Khandpur S.C., Guha D.K., Bhargava S., Aortic Aneurysm In Childhood. Chest (USA). 58, No. 2, 164, 1970.
38. Tandon B.N., Lakshiminarayana R., Bhargava S., Nayak N.C., Sama S.K., Ultrastructure of the Liver in Non-cirrhotic Portal Fibrosis with Portal Hypertension, Gut. 11, 905–10, 1970.
39. Bapna B.C., Bhargava S., Lower Urinary Obstructive Uropathy in Infancy and Childhood (Clinical Grand Round), Bull. AIIMS. 4, No. 3, 184–5, 1970.
40. Ahuja M.M.S., Sridhar C.B., Sarla P.K., Bhargava S., Metabolic Bone Disease (Osteomalacia and Osteoporosis) Clinical Grand Round, Bull. AIIMS. 4, No. 3, 187–8, 1970.

1971

41. Bhargava S., Bapna B.C., Diagnosis of Urethral Valves, Ind. Jr. Radiol. XXV, No. 2, 102–8, 1971.
42. Rajani M., Bhargava S., Achalasia of the Oesophagus in Childhood, Ind. Jr. Radiol, XXV, No. 2, 144–6, 1971.
43. Sama S.K., Bhargava S., Gopinath N., Talwar J.R., Nayak N.C., Tandon B.N., Wig K.L., Non-cirrhotic Portal Fibrosis, Am. Jr. Med. 51, No. 2, 160–9, 1971.
44. Khanna P., Bhargava S., Roentgen Assessment of Bone Density in North Indian Population, Ind. Jr. Med. Res. 59, No. 10, 1599–609, 1971.

1972

45. Berry M., Bhargava S., Roentgen Spectrum of Osseous Lesions in Multiple Myeloma, Ind. Jr. Radiol. XXVI, No. 2, 123–8, 1972.

1973

46. Berry M., Krishan A., Bhargava S., An Aneurysmal Bone Cyst of the Mandible, Ind. Jr. Radiol. XVII, No. 2, 196–8, 1973.
47. Sridhar C.B., Ram B.K., Sunder A.S.R., Bhargava S., Prakash A., Kapoor M.M., Ahuja M.M.S., Primary Hyperparathyroidism: A Clinical, Biochemical and Radiological Profile with Emphasis on Geographical Variation, Australas. Radiol. XVII, No. 2, 199–204, 1973.
48. Prusty S., Bhargava S., Talwar J.R., Chopra P., Rao I.M., Venugopal P., Patwardham R., Gopinath N., Mediastinal Tumours and Cysts, Int. Surg. 58, No. 11, 775–9, 1973.

1974

49. Khurana U., Berry M., Bhargava S., Parentral Neostfrnine in the Study of Small Bowel, Ind. Jr. Radiol. XXVIII, No. 3, 177–81, 1974.

50. Bose A., Bhargava S., Sacral Agenesis and Dysgenesis, Ind. Jr. Radiol. XXVIII, 4, 281–5, 1974.

1975

51. Kaushik D., Bhargava S., Berry M., Tandon B.M., Bhatia M.L., Hepatic Venography, Ind. Jr. Radiol. XXIV, No. 1, 16–23, 1975.
52. Rao M., Bhargava S., Pachy Demoperiostosis, Ind. Jr. Radiol. XXIV, No. 3, 204–6, 1975.
53. Bhargava S., The Peripheral Veins. Dr. Diwan Chand Memorial Oration, 1975, Ind. Jr. Radiol. XXIX, No. 4, 240–52, 1975.
54. Verma I.C., Bhargava S., Connective Tissue Disorders: Birth Defects, Original Article Series. An Autosomal Recessive Form of Lethal Chondrodystrophy with Severe Thoracic Polydactyl and Genital Anomalies. Original article series. XI, No. 6, 167, 1975.

1976

55. Tandon R.K., Gupta O.K., Kaushik D., Bhargava S., Osteolytic Lesions in Primary Systemic Amyloidosis, Jr. Asso. Phys. Ind. 24, 191–4, 1976.
56. Shrivastava S., Bhargava S., Tandon R., Partial Anomalous Pulmonary Venous Connection with Intact and Atrial Septum and Mitral Stenosis, Ind. Heart. Jr. 28, No. 3, 145–51, 1976.
57. Agarwal N., Saraya L., Bhadury R., Bhargava S., Hingorani V., Cinematographic Study with Extra Amniotic Injection of 15-Me PGF2, Contraception. 14, No. 1, 1976.
58. S. Venkataraman, Bhargava S., Virmani V., Cerebrovascular Accidents: Clinical and Radiological Features, Jr. AIIMS. 2, 159–66, 1976.
59. Tandon R.K., Tandon B.N., Tandon H.D., Bhatia M.L., Bhargava S., Lal P., Arora R.B. Study of an Epidemic of Venoocclusive Disease in India, Gut. 17, 849–55, 1976.

1977

60. Khurana J.S., Bhargava S., Tandon P.N., Posterior Fossa Mass Lesions: A Study of 100 Cases (Part II), Ind. Jr. Radiol. 31, No. 2, 114–16, 1977.

1978

61. Kumar R., Bhargava S., Increase in the Detection Probability by Collywobbling, Jr. AIIMS. 4, No. 2, 170–3, 1978.
62. Berry M., Narendranathan M., Rajani M., Bhargava S. Chiba Needle Cholangiography in Hepato-biliary Diseases, Australas. Radiol. 22, No. 2, 139–44, 1978.
63. Malaviya A.N., Mehra N.K., Bhargava S., Adhar G.C., Jindal K., Seronergative Spondarthritis Diagnostic Help from Tissue Typing, Jr. AIIMS. 3, 254–9, 1978.

1979

64. Mukhopadhyay S., Bhargava S., Sood N.N., The Techniques of Macrodacryocystography and Normal Anatomy and of Nasolacmal Passage, (Part I), Ind. Jr. Radiol. XXXIII, No. 1, 8–10, 1979.
65. Mukhopadhyay S., Bhargava S., Sood N.N., Macrodacryocystography as an Aid in the Management of Epiphora (Part II), Ind. Jr. Radiol. XXXIII, No. 1, 11–14, 1979.
66. Bhargava S., Atib M.H., Early Rheumatoid Arthritis Evaluated by Ball-Catching View, Ind. Jr. Radiol. XXXIII, No. 1, 15–20, 1979.
67. Malaviya A.N., Mehra N.K., Adhar G.C., Jindal K., Bhargava S., Batta R.K., Vaidya M.C., Tandon R.K., Sankaran, B.P, The Clinical Spectrum of HLA-B27 Related Rheumatic Diseases in India, Jr. Asso. Phys. Ind. 27, No. 6, 487–92, 1979.
68. Malaviya A.N., Mehra N.K., Adhar G.C., Jindal K., Bhargava S., Batta R.K., Tandon R.K. Seronegative Spondyathritis

Syndrome. Clinical, Immunological and Genetic Patterns, Aspects of Allergy, Appl. Immunol. XII, 147–50, 1979.
69. Berry M., Bhardwaj V.N., Bhargava S. Hypotonic Tubeless Duodenography, Ind. Jr. Radiol. 33, 189–97, 1979.
70. Bhargava S., CAT Scanner Proves Invaluable in Diagnosis of Brain Disease, Medical Times, Nov. 1979.

1980

71. Bhargava S., Intracranial Tuberculosis, Ind. Jr. Radiol. XXXIV, No. 1, 1–3, 1980.
72. Kumar R., Bhargava S., Hardware Image Artifacts in CT Imaging, AMPI Med. Physics Bull. 15, No. 2, 28–30, 1980.
73. Bhargava S., Intracranial Tuberculosis: Editorial, Ind. Jr. Radiol. XXXIV, No. 1, 1980.
74. Mukhopadhyay S., Bhargava S., Angiography in Pheochromocytoma, lnd. Jr. Radiol. XXIV, No. 147, 1980.
75. Bhargava S., Tandon P.N., lntracranial Tuberculosis: A CT Study, British Jr. Radiol. 53, 935–45, 1980.
76. Rao M., Goulatia R.K., Bhargava S., CT Analysis of the 1st 525 Patients, Neurol. Ind. 28, No. 2, 86–95, 1980.
77. Rajani M., Shrivastava S., Tandon R., Bhargava S., Right Ventricular Cineangiography in Tetralogy of Fallot, Cardiovasc. lntervent. Radiol. 3, No. 1, 13–17, 1980.

1981

78. Wani M.A., Banerjee A.K., Tandon P.N., Bhargava S., Neurocysticercosis. Some Uncommon Presentations, Neurol. lnd. XXIX, No. 2, 58–63, 1981.
79. Gothi R., Bhargava S., Pycnodysotosis. A Report of 3 Cases, Ind. Jr. Radiol. XXV, No. 199, 1981.
80. Rajani M., Tandon R., Bhargava S., Angiography in Ruptured Sinus of Valsalva Fistula, Ind. Jr. Radiol. 35, No. 4, 257–62, 1981.
81. Bazaz R., Bhargava S., CT Scan in Neuropediatrics, Ind. Jr. Pediat. 48, 249–54, 1981.

82. Bazaz R., Bhargava S., Radiology of Hirschsprung's Disease, Ind. Jr. Radiol. 36, 25–9, 1981.

1982

83. Bhargava S., Gupta A.K., Tandon P.N., Tubercular Meningitis: A CT Study, Br. Jr. Radiol. 55, No. 3, 1982.
84. Chopra U., Datta R.K., Dasgupta A., Bhargava S., Non-specific Aortoarteritis: Immunologic Study of 50 Cases. Jpn Heart journal. July : 24 (4) : 549–56. DoI: 101536/ihj24.549.
85. Chandra P., Bhargava S., Dhawan I.K., Angiography in Potential Live Kidney Donors, Ind. Jr. Surg. 44, 2, 1982.
86. Wani M.A., Tandon P.N., Banerjee A.K., Bhargava S., Intraventricular Cysticercosis, Neurol. Ind. XXX, No. 3, 157–62, 1982.
87. Upadhyaya P., Bhargava S., Results in Ventriculoarterial Surgery for Hydrocephalus using Indian Shunt Valve, Jr. Progress Ped. Surg. Vol.15, 209–22, 1982.
88. Bhat V.S., Mukhopadhya S., Bhargava S., Roentgen Changes in Thoracic Cage in CHD, Ind. Jr. Radial. Imaging. 37, No. 2, 129–34, 1982.
89. Sridharan R., Berry M., Bhargava S., Changes in Excretory System in Mullerian Duct Failure, Ind. Jr. Radiol. 36, 4, 1982.
90. Bhargava S., Advances in Medical Imaging, CT, US, MRI and Digital Imaging, First US India Radiology Conference, 1982.

1983

91. Chopra P., Dasgupta A., Bhargava S., Non-specific Aortoarteritis: (Takayasu's Disease). An Immunologic and Autopsy Study, Japanese Heart Jr. 24, No. 4, 549–56, 1983.
92. Prakash S., Mehra N.K., Bhargava S., Malaviya A.N., Reiter's Disease in Northern India: A Clinical and Immunogenetic Study, Rheumatol. Int. 3, 101–4, 1983.

93. Prakash S., Mehra N.K., Bhargava S., Malaviya A.N., HLA-B27 Related, 'Unclassifiable' Seronegative Spondyloarthropathies, Ann. Rheumatol. Dis. 42, 640–3, 1983.
94. Prakash S., Gopinath P.G., Bhargava S., Mehra N.K., Malaviya A.N., Evaluation of Quantitative Sacroiliac Scintigraphy for the Early Detection of Sacroilietis, Eur. Jr. Nucl. Med. 8, 531–4, 1983.
95. Prakash S., Bhargava S., Mehra N.K., Malaviya A.N., HLA B27 Related 'Unclassifiable' Seronegative Spondyloarthropathies, Ann. Rheumatol. Dis. 4200, 111–14, 1983.
96. Kashyap N., Nundy S., Bhargava S., Evaluation of Techniques for Assessing Portosystemic Shunt Patency, Ind. Jr. Med. Res. 78, 841–6, 1983.
97. Gupta A., Bhargava S., Posterior Mediastinal Mass, Ind. Jr. Chest Dis. Allied Sc. April–June, 141–4, 1983.
98. Bhargava S., Radiology Including CT of Parasitic Disease of the Central Nervous System, Neurosurg. Rev. 6, 129–37, 1983.
99. Rajani M., Mukhopadhyay S., Maheshwari R., Venugopal P., Bhargava S. Thrombosis of Björk—Shiley Valve Prostheses: Evaluation by Cineradiography, Acta Radiol. Diagnosis, 24, No. 5, 36–7, 1983.
100. Bhargava S., Maheshwari M.C., CT Evaluation in Peripartum Stroke, Clin. Radiol. 1983. Volume 34. Issue No. 6, 633–37.
101. Malhotra K.K., Sharma R.K., Pradhakar S., Bhargava S., Aortoarteritis as a Major Cause of Renovascular Hypertension in the Young, Ind. Jr. Med. Res. 77, 487–94, 1983.
102. Upadhyaya P., Bhargava S., Sundaram K.R., Mitra D.K., Hydrocephalus Caused by Tubercular Meningitis Clinical Picture, CT Findings and Results of Shunt Surgery, Z. Kinderchir. 38, Supplement II, 76–9, 1983.

1984

103. Bhargava S., Biona, Bazaz R., Roentgen Evaluation of Abdominal Masses in Children, Ind. Jr. Radiol. 37, 4, 1984.

1985

104. Vashisht S., Goulatia R.K., Dayal Y., Bhargava S., Radiological Evaluation of Mucoceles of the Paranasal Sinuses, Br. Jr. Radiol. 58, 959–63, 1985.
105. Tandon P.N., Bhargava S., Effect of Medical Treatment on Intracranial Tuberculomas: CT Study, Tubercle. 66, 86-97, 1985.

1986

106. Berry M., Bazaz R., Bhargava S., Amoebic Liver Abscess: Sonographic Diagnosis and Management, Jr. Clin. Ultrasound. Texas. 14, No. 4, 239-42, 1986.
107. Rajani M., Mukhopadhyay S., Maheshwari R., Iyer, Venugopal P., Bhargava S., Cine-fluororadiographic Evaluation of the Björk-Shiley Prosthesis: A Serial Post-operative Follow-up in 400 Patients, Australas. Radiol. 30, No. 1, 13–18, 1986.
108. Bhargava S., Tandon P.N., CNS Tuberculosis Lessons Learnt from CT Studies, Neurol. Ind. 28, No. 4, 208–12, 1986.
109. Gupta A.K., Bhargava S., Rohatgi M., Anal Agenesis with Recto-bulbar Fistula, Paed. Radiol. 16, 22–5, 1986.
110. Rajani M., Mukhopadhyay S., Maheshwari R., Iyer, Venugopal P., Bhargava S. Cine-fluororadiographic Evaluation of the Björk-Shiley Prosthesis: A Serial Post-operative Follow-up in 400 Patients, Australas. Radiol. 30, No. 1, 13–18, 1986.
111. Vashisht S., Goulatia R.K., Dayal Y., Bhargava S., Orbital Lesions: A CT Study, Ind. Jr. Radiol. Imag. 40, No. 4, 249–55, 1986.
112. Iyengar J.K., Rohatgi M., Menon P.S.N., Mathews A.R., Verma I.C., Bhargava S., Clinical, Cytogenetic and Hormonal Profile in Extreme Hypospadias with Bilateral Descanted Testes, Ind. Jr. Med. Res. 83, 604–9, 1986.
113. Vashisht S., Goulatia R.K., Dayal Y., Bhargava S., Orbito Facial Neurofibromatosis: A CT Study, Afro-Asian Jr. Ophthalmol. 1, 11–14, 1986.

1987

114. Gupta A.K., Bhargava S., Bladder Hemangioma: Ultrasonographic Demonstration, Urol. Radiol. 31, 281–6, 1987.
115. Gupta A.K., Berry M., Bhargava S., Atypical Target Pattern: Sonography in GIT Lesions, Australas. Radiol. 31, 281–6, 1987.
116. Verma A., Maheshwari M.C., Bhargava S., Spontaneous Intraventricular Haemorrhage, Jr. Neurol. 234, 233–6, 1987.
117. Vashisht S., Gupta A., Mathur M., Bhargava S., An Abdominal Echinococcal Cyst Communicating with the Pancreatic Duct: An Unusual Presentation, Ind. Jr. Radiol. Imag. 41, 33–5, 1987.
118. Gupta A.K., Berry M., Bhargava S. Sonographic Double Target in a Case of Type Ia Caecal Duplication Cyst, Jr. Clin. Ultrasound. 15, 273–5, 1987.

1988

119. Gupta A.K., Bhargava S., Juvenile Xanthogranuloma with Pulmonary Lesions, Ped. Radiol. 18, 70–4, 1988.
120. Sood M., Hingorani V., Kashyap N.K., Kumar S., Berry M., Bhargava S., Ultrasonic Measurements of Foetal Parameters in Normal Pregnancy and in Intrauterine Growth Retardation, Ind. Jr. Med. Res. 87, 453–8, 1988.
121. Kaul M., Khosla A., Rajani M., Bhargava S. Metacarpal Index in Normal Adult Indian Population, Ind. Jr. Med. Res. 87, 293–7, 1988.
122. Seth V., Mukhopadhyay S., Bhargava S., Tuberculosis in Children: A Broad Overview, Nat. Med. Jr. Ind. 1988.
123. Rajani M., Mukhopadhyay S., Dogra B., Shrivastava S., Bhatia M.L., Bhargava S., Primary Cardiac Masses: A Study of 24 Cases, Australas. Radiol. 32, 84–91, 1988.

1989

124. Bhargava S. et al., Choledocholithiasis: An Ultrasonic Study with Comparative Evaluation with ERCP/PTC, Australas. Radiol. 32, 220–6, 1989.

1991

125. Bhargava S., The Continuing Challenge of Preventable Cancer in India, Proceedings of the Clinical Oncology Society. 1991.
126. Bhargava S., Impact of the New Imaging Technologies in Developing Countries, Proceeding of Asian Oceanic Congress of Radiology. 1991.
127. Bhargava S., The History of the Indian Radiological Association, Proceeding of Asian Oceanic Congress of Radiology. 1991.

1992

128. Bhargava S., Radiology & Imaging: Past, Present & Future, Annals of the National Academy of Medical Sciences, 1994.

1995

129. Bhargava S., Iyer P.S., X-rays in Medicine in India: The Early Days, Ind. Jr. Radiol. 1995.
130. Bhargava S., The Ethics of New Technology: 100 Years of Radiological Sciences, World Health. No. 3, 1995.

1996

131. Bhargava S., Watmough D.J., Syed F., Menon A., Gharbawy F., High Detection Rates Do Not Necessarily Lead to Lower Mortality, BMJ. 312, 1996.

1997

132. Bhargava S., Tuberculosis of the Parotid Gland: A CT Study, Br. Jr. Radiol. 1997.
133. Malaviya A.N., Sehab D., Bhargava S., Characteristics of Osteoarthritis among Kuwaitis: A Hospital-Based Study, Clin. Rheumatol.,1997.

1998

134. Bhargava S., WHO Technical Report Series 857: Training in Diagnostic US: Essential Principles & Standards, 1998.

Chapters in Textbooks

1. Radiology of Neurocysticercosis Progress, in *Clinical Medicine in India*, M.M.S. Ahuja and Arnold Heinemamm (eds), New Delhi.
2. An Evaluation of 4 Methods for Assessing Patency or Portal Systemic Shunts, in *Portal Hypertension in India*, S. Nundy and B.N. Tandon (eds).
3. Imaging of the Heart; and Great Vessels, in *Clinical Medicine*, M.L. Bhatia (ed.), Association of Physician of India.
4. Radiology Including CT of Neurocysticercosis, in *Neurosurgical Review* H.W. Pia, K. Sano, Vo.6 1983, No.3 Publishers Walter de Gruyter, Berlin N.Z.
5. Chapter 22: CT in Intracranial Neurotuberculosis, in *Neurosciences in the Tropics*, D.K. Dastur et al (eds).
6. Imaging Technologies for Developing Countries, in WHO Technical Series Publication, Geneva. Expert group members.
7. Algorithms in Radiologic Diagnosis, in WHO Technical Series Publication, Geneva. Expert group members. 1988.

Appendix B

Awards and Honours

- Awarded the Padma Shri by the President of India for my contribution to medical education and medical service in 1991.
- Radiologist to the President of India, Neelam Sanjiva Reddy, from 1978 to 1990.

Professional Honours

- FNAMS: Fellow of the National Academy of Medical Sciences
- FICRI: Fellow of the Indian College of Radiology & Imaging. 1982.
- FNASI: Fellow of the National Academy of Sciences India. 1984.
- FRCR: Fellow of the Royal College of Radiologist, London. 1984.
- FACR: Fellow of the American College of Radiology. 2021.
- Honorary member, Radiological Society of North America (RSNA). 2018.

Doctorates

- DSc Honoris Causa, Sanjay Gandhi Post Graduate Institute of Medical Sciences, Lucknow
- DSc Honoris Causa, Jabalpur University, Jabalpur

Chair of National and International Committees

- Chair of the WHO Advisory Committee on Health Research for the Southeast Asia region
- Advisor to the Radiation Medicine Group of WHO Geneva
- Chair of Advisory Committee for Medical Books, National Book Trust
- Convener of the Specialty Board for Radio-Diagnosis of the National Board of Examinations, New Delhi
- Chair of the Governing Board of the Vallabh Bhai Patel Chest Institute, University of Delhi
- Chair, Scientific Exhibition of the twentieth International Conference of Radiology in New Delhi
- Chair, Science and Technology for Women, Department of Science and Technology, Ministry of Science and Technology, Government of India
- Chair of the Telemedicine Committee of the Medical Council of India.

Chair of Ethics Committees

- Medical Council of India
- Centre for Policy Research, New Delhi
- The Energy and Resources Institute (TERI)
- Batra Hospital and Research Centre
- Dharamshila Cancer Hospital and Research Centre
- Apothecaries Ltd (independent ethics committee)

Lifetime Achievement Awards

- AIIMS awarded by Prime Minister Narendra Modi, 2014
- International Society of Radiology, awarded by Atal Bihari Vajpayee, 1998

- Millennium Award by the Indian Radiological Imaging Association, 2000
- Swasth Bharat Samman by Zee TV

Orations: National and International

National
- Om Prakash Bhasin Oration for Medical Sciences, 1997
- Diwan Chand Aggarwal Memorial Oration, Indian Radiology and Imaging Association, 1976
- Thingram Memorial Oration, Railways Medical Association, 1981
- MN Sen Oration of the Indian Council of Medical Research, 1984
- Glaxo Oration of the National Academy of Medical Sciences, 1985
- Shurvir Singh Medical Oration, Medical College Udaipur, 1987
- Prof. Kumar Memorial Oration, King George's Medical University, Lucknow, 1987
- Brig. S.K. Mazumdar Memorial Trust Oration, 1988
- NASI Oration

International
- 'Tuberculomas of the Brain: A CT Study', Karolinska Institute Stockholm
- 'Ultrasound of AN Amebic Liver Abscess', European Ultrasound Society, Herlev
- 'Neurocysticercosis' International Society of Radiology, Brussels
- 'Tuberculosis of the Spine', Tufts Medical Centre, Boston. 1972.

Visiting Professorships

- Postgraduate Institute of Medical Education and Research, Chandigarh
- Sanjay Gandhi Postgraduate Institute of Medical Sciences, Lucknow
- Shri Chitratrinool Institute, Thiruvananthapuram
- Center of Cellular and Molecular Biology, Hyderabad

Appendix C

How Others Saw Me

Over a long career, I have interacted with people from all walks of life and of all ages and backgrounds. I have seen unsure and callow students grow up to become top doctors heading departments. Some individuals I spent many years working with have died. But here are some testimonials from a handful of all the people who crossed my path or worked closely with me.

Mahesh Chandra Misra
Former Director, AIIMS; Presently Senior Consultant Surgeon, Sitaram Bhartia Institute of Science and Research, New Delhi

I joined AIIMS as a senior resident in surgery in 1980. It was a dream come true. I was posted in casualty (presently the Department of Emergency Medicine) for a year. Professor Sneh Bhargava was the chairperson of the Hospital Management Board and a renowned radiologist. She was not only head of the prestigious Department of Radio Diagnosis, she was also responsible for running AIIMS.

I had heard a great deal about her professional competence and skills as a radiologist. Her administrative acumen was also well-known, along with her forthrightness and disciplined approach. Her command of radiodiagnosis reporting made even senior surgeons blush. During my one year in casualty, we used to have weekly meetings with Dr A.N. Safaya to discuss issues, and that is when I first encountered Professor Bhargava's expertise as the authority in India on conventional diagnostic modalities. At these weekly conferences, everyone present appreciated her sense of humour and how she pulled the leg of senior surgical faculty while giving her forensic analysis of imaging films with just one glance. There was a legendary story about how her imaging acumen led her to a diagnosis of lung cancer for President Neelam Sanjiva Reddy based on a simple chest X-ray. As it was caught early, President Reddy lived a normal life for many years and died in 1996 at the age of 83.

She was famous for her commitment, uncompromising character and prompt decisions. She was a woman of action who could not tolerate inefficiency, and this made some people scared of her and others full of admiration. Thanks to her, AIIMS was the first hospital in the country to get a CT head machine in 1977 and an ultrasound machine in1981. This enabled future generations to understand and learn about the ultrasound morphology of body organs and tissues. As a badge of honour for her commitment, decisiveness, professional excellence and leadership qualities, Professor Bhargava was selected as the first woman director of AIIMS in 1984 in one of Prime Minister Indira Gandhi's most important appointments prior to her assassination. In her first week, Professor Bhargava had to handle not only the assassination but also the victims of the anti-Sikh riots who flocked to AIIMS Casualty as patients. The Bhopal gas tragedy followed, pushing the Institute's resources to the limit.

AIIMS witnessed tremendous growth and development under her dynamic leadership. The cardiothoracic centre, the neurosciences centre and the Institute Rotary Cancer Hospital were established under her leadership, besides several new departments, academic programmes and computerization. We, as young faculty at that time, were greatly inspired by her constant striving for perfection. Thanks to her focus on providing faculty with housing, which she had organized in the late 1980s and early '90s, I was able to enjoy living in a flat in the Asiad Games Village for three years.

I feel privileged to be able to share my thoughts of this towering personality and pray for her continued healthy life. She remains an icon of outstanding healthcare.

Dr Renu Gupta
Assistant Professor, AIIMS, current professor of radiology, Kuwait University

I feel extremely privileged to share my memories of Professor Sneh Bhargava. I have known her since 1986, when I joined the department of radiology at AIIMS as a senior resident. At that time, I had just returned from Oxford where I was trained in radiology as a Siemens scholar. I was excited at the prospect of working at the topmost medical institution in the country under the guidance of Dr Bhargava as I had heard a lot about her while doing my residency at Postgraduate Institute of Medical Education and Research, Chandigarh, and in the UK. Since then, she has been my mentor, guide and guru. I was subsequently selected as faculty at AIIMS and worked with Dr Bhargava until her retirement.

I vividly recall my first meeting with her in her office on joining AIIMS. She was both director and head of radiology. She was seated behind her desk in a cotton sari, looking very impressive and authoritative. Her short, grey hair suited her, and the glasses hanging around her neck on a golden chain added grace to her academic, scholarly looks. Without wasting any time, she asked me why I had returned to India from Oxford and why AIIMS. I told her honestly that I came back because of family reasons and thought there was no better place for training and pursuing my dreams than working under her.

It is not only in India that Dr Bhargava is admired and respected as a radiologist. She is admired throughout the radiology fraternity abroad too and is famous for her contributions to teaching, training and research. To get the opportunity to work with her and learn from her was the ambition of many radiology residents, and I was lucky to get that opportunity.

Working with Dr Bhargava taught me not only the in-depth medical aspects of radiology but the administrative side of how to conduct meetings, arrange conferences and organize teaching activities. She is highly disciplined, organized and focussed – the essential qualities of a truly able medical and administrative professional.

She was also fully involved with her 'baby' – the radiology department that she had built up and developed. Everything in the department was efficiently organized, and she was personally involved, starting with early morning meetings, afternoon teaching seminars, journal clubs and ongoing research. The grilling I went through while working with her over two years laid the foundation of my future career. All the residents were kept on their toes due to her no-nonsense approach and knowledge. No one could ever match her energy level, enthusiasm and administrative capabilities.

Besides being the top radiologist in the country, Dr Bhargava is a wonderful, caring, supportive, affectionate and humble human being who also found time to involve herself at a personal level with her staff and students. She had a problem-solving attitude and vision for the future. She is also blessed with an exceptionally good memory.

At the workplace, every minute was precious for Dr Bhargava. This unwavering devotion to work was very noticeable daily when Mr Arjun Singh, head of technologists and the backbone of the department, had to run to keep up with the pace of Dr Bhargava while noting down daily administrative matters as he walked with her from the radiology department to her office. Arjun Singh worked for many years in the radiology department under her leadership. AIIMS was visited by highly placed government functionaries, members of Parliament (MPs), and ministers, and Arjun Singh would manage all these pressures at work amicably without disturbing the normal routine.

Dr Bhargava standardized the station-wise working protocols and teaching protocols for the department. These are followed to this day. The morning teaching meetings that she introduced were unique, and everyone present was able to learn a great deal from every case she reviewed. It was a joy to watch, except when you were in the hot seat and had to face her questions while presenting a case. She would randomly visit workstations to check. I remember, one day she passed by the corridor where I was injecting patients for IVPs and waiting for the technologist to bring the films to decide if anyone needed delayed films. She told me not to wait but to go to the dark room myself to see the films and decide. I followed that habit till the end of my residency and it saved so much time for patients and technologists.

When I joined AIIMS, there were many technical advances coming up in radiology. Dr Bhargava had developed the department since its inception and continued the pace for technical modernization as well as changing the requirements in teaching and expertise. As faculty, she wanted me to work with upcoming imaging modalities. At that time, she was planning to open an MRI centre and suggested that I should train in using MRI as an imaging tool as well as for research in spectroscopy and functional MRI. Following her advice, I submitted a project in MRI spectroscopy training, which was approved by the Department of Science and Technology. She arranged a spot for me at National Institutes of Health, Bethesda, USA, to train in the field as a Boyscast Fellow. This is a perfect example of how she always had her eye on training staff for upcoming fields before starting any new facilities. She was also instrumental in the planning and starting of new subspecialities like cardiac, neuro, cancer and trauma centres at AIIMS, which provide world-class radiology facilities in training and patient care in the country.

Post retirement from AIIMS, Kuwait University invited her to establish a radiology department, and she impressed the top personnel in its faculty of medicine with her competence, professionalism and administrative capabilities.

To me, Dr Bhargava is a highly professional, brilliant radiologist and an excellent teacher who has contributed enormously to the field of radiology. I feel privileged and proud to have been trained by such a magnanimous personality as Dr Bhargava. She faced many struggles and administrative obstacles at AIIMS, but she stood strong to keep the interests of the institute foremost. Dr Sneh Bhargava, you are greatly admired, loved and revered by all of us.

Dr Rajesh Gothi
MD, AIIMS, former student, radiology

It was while doing house jobs in neurosurgery and orthopaedic surgery at AIIMS that I came across Professor Bhargava. Our neuro and ortho conferences were steered by her and were probably the most interesting part of the day. There was learning, discussion and great interaction between the various teachers and residents. It was impressive, and learning from her was something for me to consider in the future. When the day to complete junior residency and study towards postgraduation arrived, I was asked to consider the five-year MS neurosurgery course at NIMHANS, Bangalore. In fact, I was to join NIMHANS in three months. In the interim, not knowing what to do for three months, I took the entrance test for MD radiology. The result was surreal. The stars were probably aligned in my favour. Out of the 40 students who sat for that one 'general' category seat, I was chosen. My first day started with following Madam [Professor Bhargava] to the autopsy room in the basement of the hospital. There, Dr Purshottam Upadhyaya, professor of paediatric surgery, was performing a limited autopsy of a baby. Madam kept prodding him to look beyond what he had already dissected. In sheer exasperation, he ended up saying: 'Actually there is no need to do the autopsy, Sneh has already told us everything beforehand.'

In another incident, Professor S. Nundy, made a comment that in AIIMS, there are very few people who actually make a diagnosis and Dr Bhargava is one of them. The course was a truly enjoyable learning experience and when I finished with the MD, she advised me never to forget the library. To this day, I look up to her whenever the need arises. She is just not a teacher but also a guru, and nothing can repay the debt that we students owe her.

Professor H.P.S. Sachdev
MD, FRCPCH, FAMS, FIAP, former AIIMS student, pediatrics

As young undergraduates at AIIMS, we only had occasional direct interactions with the radiology department. This exposure increased when, as interns, we attended the weekly radiology conferences of the various specialities. I was thoroughly impressed by Professor Sneh Bhargava's clarity of thoughts and the insistence on getting the full patient history before imparting her radiological opinion. There were instances when she would ask relevant clinical questions, which proved embarrassing for the clinicians who had overlooked these aspects. Invariably, her opinion proved to be spot-on or a pointer towards the correct direction.

Subsequently, as postgraduate students, we had to present our cases to her in the radiology conference. Thus, we had to be very thorough in eliciting clinical history, a habit that is yielding rich dividends now. Her scolding, followed by gentle teaching of the radiological findings, was a noteworthy trademark. The poster in her room stating, 'The eyes see what the mind knows', has been imprinted in my mind. An avid reader of evidence, she was always open to the latest technological advances. During her tenure, AIIMS got the first CT scanner in the country.

Thirty-five years after leaving AIIMS, I was fortunate enough to again be mentored by her at the Sitaram Bhartia Institute of Science and Research. As she was the medical director, I was exposed to her plethora of skills, particularly her leadership qualities. She practised astute administration, going into the minutest of details, interacting with all the stakeholders, including doctors, nurses and paramedical staff, maintenance and administrative staff, pursuing the tasks till successful completion. She never compromised on ethical values.

Professor Bhargava provided support to all the specialities in a balanced manner without fear or favour. She is always willing to learn and, even in her nineties, made it a point to come to the weekly continuing medical education (CMEs) and make pertinent comments. Her perpetual quest for improvement is a noteworthy quality, which rubs off on colleagues. Despite age-related physical constraints, her razor-sharp thinking is still full of clarity.

Her humane and socializing qualities surfaced during tea clubs and institutional social functions where, even in her nineties, she would dance with the nursing staff. Her anecdotes from the yesteryears, laced with humour and wit, would keep us spellbound at the tea club. She invariably participated in the occasions of joy and family bereavement of colleagues. She was a perfect host at home too. On a personal level, she offered valuable advice and was always willing to help out if she could.

I feel privileged for being mentored by this iconic personality and pray to the Almighty for her continued healthy life.

Former AIIMS Students

Dr J. Maheshwari

I remember her as a dynamic lady-professor, walking down the corridors of AIIMS with the 'tak-tak' sound of her heels. She was short in stature but imposing owing to the force of her personality and commitment to high standards. I was always very enamoured with her knowledge and authoritative demeanour.

Her powers of diagnosis were remarkable. At one of our morning conferences, we looked at the X-rays of one elderly person admitted with back pain. We had done all possible tests but were not able to come to a diagnosis. Professor Bhargava looked at the films and asked our professor and head, 'Pradeep, have you done a per rectum (PR) on him?'. We giggled at the idea of how an orthopaedic surgeon would do a PR. We called a urologist who did a PR and a needle biopsy of the prostate. It was prostate cancer.

When she was director at AIIMS, the sign on her desk read: 'Come to me with a problem with at least two possible solutions'. Her favourite line on top of the view boxes was 'The Eye sees what the Mind knows.'

One time, she walked into the paediatric ward during a radiology meeting, took one look at the chest X-ray and said, 'Wrong film.' We were stunned. She pointed out that it was unlikely for an 18-year-old male to have breast shadows. None of us had noticed. We chuckled to ourselves later that she was also Sherlock Holmes.

Dr Bhargava is an elegant lady, a brilliant mind, brilliant speaker and a fantastic head of department and director. A very strong person. However, if I were her, I would be more flexible, approachable and not demanding. After all, no one is perfect.

AIIMS Student

My frank critique of her after having the pleasure of working under her for close to two years after her retirement:
1. Excellent host at her residence
2. Doesn't shy from calling a spade a spade in private, including calling me fat
3. Always a student of radiology
4. Very approachable if you have relevance
5. Her better half was a great bridge player and she had a room for playing bridge at their residence in New Friends Colony.
6. She superseded many, many men to become director at AIIMS and yet they still treated her with respect.
7. For those who are unaware, Indira Gandhi used to admire her, and her appointment as director was one of the first files that Rajiv Gandhi signed.

AIIMS Student

Excellent radiologist. Probably the best conventional radiologist alive and a great student of evolving radiology. No one can match her. In 1984, I showed her an X-ray brought by me from Benghazi in Libya, and the moment she saw it, she said 'ectopic kidney'. I was mesmerized. I had the opportunity to be associated with her at Dharamshila Cancer Hospital. Her brilliance in radiology always shone. As an individual, very sharp but very congenial. We would have tea together on most days, chat, share jokes.

AIIMS Student

She once quoted a line of poetry to me: *Paisa Khuda toh nahi, par Khuda ki kasam, Khuda se kam nahi* (Money is not God, but I swear it God, it's no less than God). Dr Sneh Bhargava has a personality to be reckoned with. She exudes an aura of confidence and virtue. So dignified that she commands instant respect. I touch her feet when I meet her, an instinctive gesture of respect.

Pragyaya
Department of Quality, Sitaram Bhartia Institute of Science and Research

Dr Sneh Bhargava ma'am is a role model for any healthcare professional. She is a strong lady who embodies the qualities of leadership, advocacy, resilience and compassion. As part of her focus on patient safety, she used to take daily rounds of wards, and during these rounds, she encouraged the nurses to be empowered and knowledgeable about all conditions related to the assigned patient. This was to ensure that they could confidently take complete charge of their patient. She has always been a guide and mentor during her rounds. Sometimes tough, sometimes soft, she knows how to balance the string and prevent it from breaking.

Her sole passion is to provide quality care for patients. Her leadership is characterized by unwavering diligence, as she has consistently demonstrated an exceptional commitment to her responsibilities and to the well-being of her team. Through her tireless efforts and attention to detail, she has always ensured that the tasks are completed efficiently, effectively and, most importantly, timely. As a diligent leader and motivator, she leads by example, fostering a culture of accountability and achievement. Her dedication to continuous improvement and excellence inspires those around her to strive for their best. Her meticulous approach can best be seen in the fact that even when documents are prepared for auditors, she has them proofread to ensure there are no mistakes. This attention to detail reflects her commitment to excellence and reinforces her reputation as a diligent leader who takes pride in delivering high quality work.

Despite her age, she remains remarkably active and serves as a motivating force for patients during her rounds. Her vibrant energy and positive demeanour uplift those who are tired of illness, instilling in them a sense of hope.

Her dedication towards the organization, the work and team building is unparalleled as she wholeheartedly participates in all the activities, whether it's CMEs, birthday celebrations or Diwali get-togethers. By embracing every opportunity to contribute with her presence, she embodies the value of teamwork and collaboration, inspiring others to follow suit.

She remains steadfast in prioritizing and nurturing her health and well-being by engaging in yoga and physical fitness to maintain her vitality and strength. She always remains active and engaged during her work. Her commitment towards self-care serves as a powerful example to others, demonstrating that age is no barrier to leading a fulfilling and active lifestyle. She is an inspiration to those around her to invest in their well-being.

She embraces each day with a zest for life, living it to the fullest in every aspect. Alongside her unwavering dedication to her responsibilities, she exudes a remarkable sense of style and grace, particularly evident in her choice of attire. With an impeccable taste for fashion, she effortlessly wears lovely saris with matching accessories such as brooches and spectacle chains. Her attire reflects not only her appreciation for tradition but also her flair for modern aesthetics. To conclude, she serves as an enduring inspiration to people around her of all ages, transcending generational boundaries.

Ma'am, we consider ourselves fortunate to have had an opportunity to work with and learn alongside you, and benefit from your invaluable guidance.

Peter Johnson
Nursing Superintendent, Sitaram Bhartia Institute of Science and Research

Ma'am started her journey at Sitaram Bhartia in 1997, and the very first characteristic that everyone who came into contact with her soon learnt was that she values hard work and has been a lifelong learner. This made her accept new challenges, adapt new ideas and create new systems. Every contribution of hers helped the medical staff as well as the patients and their relatives. She thought nothing of visiting every single patient and every department workstation to get feedback and ensure that quality standards were being met. Because of how she worked to improve the performance of nurses, any doctor or relative visiting the patient would find that the nurse knew every detail, from the reasons for their admission, their medical history and current clinical condition.

Ma'am's decision-making capacity is tremendous. Whenever there was a point where the solution lay in a grey area, Ma'am always used to ask five whys and along with this she would be ready with the solution.

Ma'am was a mother and grandmother to our entire team.

As she always gives everything her maximum energy, she gives 100 per cent to celebrations and parties too. She was always on the dance floor and always having a ball.

Jitendar Nagpal
Deputy Director, Medical, Sitaram Bhartia Institute of Science and Research

I worked with Dr Bhargava for 18 years and I can only say that she has been a great leader, mentor and inspiration for me and many others in the medical field. Dr Bhargava has a very charismatic and dignified personality. She has a presence and an aura that commands respect and admiration. She has confidence and poise. She has a voice and a tone that convey clarity and conviction. She has a smile that expresses warmth and kindness. She has a style and a grace that reflects elegance and sophistication. She has a vision and a mission that inspires passion and commitment.

One of the highlights of my career was when Dr Bhargava appointed me as the head of paediatrics in 2011. I had joined the hospital as an attending consultant in 2005 and had worked hard to prove myself as a competent leader of the department. She also encouraged me to pursue further education and research in my field. I always found her supportive of my ideas and initiatives. By announcing me as the head, she showed great trust and confidence in me and I was honoured.

Another aspect of my experience with Dr Bhargava that I cherish is her narration of wise experiences. She has been in the medical field for over 60 years and has seen and done it all. She has been a pioneer in many areas of medical administration and has contributed to the advancement of medical science and practice. She has also faced many challenges and difficulties and has overcome them with courage and resilience. Dr Bhargava has a wealth of knowledge and wisdom that she generously shares with her colleagues and juniors. Whenever I had a doubt or a dilemma, I would seek her counsel and she would always have a relevant and insightful story to tell me, also using humour and anecdotes to make her point.

She does not tolerate any negligence or carelessness. She expects everyone to be diligent and meticulous in their duties and to follow the protocols and procedures. She is very particular about monthly reports and patient outcomes, hygiene and safety standards. She does not hesitate to point out any errors or lapses and I was often at the receiving end of her irritation, but I learned to take it as a sign of her high expectations and her concern for the patients and the hospital.

Dr Bhargava has earned the respect and esteem of everyone in the hospital and beyond. She has the trust and loyalty of her colleagues and subordinates. She has the appreciation and recognition of her peers and seniors. She symbolizes honour and distinction in the medical profession. This is the legacy and the impact of her work and life. Dr Bhargava has been more than a boss or a mentor to me. For me, she embodies the phrase: 'Respect is not something you demand, it is something you earn. Respect is not something you impose. It is something you inspire. Respect is not something you take; it is something you give. Respect is not something you have; it is something you are.'

She has been a part of my journey and my story and many others like me. I am grateful for my 18 years with her while knowing there must be thousands like me.

Dr Ashok Khurana

Radiologist, and Secretary, Society of Fetal Medicine, former AIIMS student, radiology

The Society of Fetal Medicine is a global forum of Indian origin that has a vision of giving every foetus an optimal outcome. At its annual convention each year, there is a 'Living Legend Sneh Bhargava Oration', which was instituted in 2006 to perpetuate the impeccable standards of a professional colleague who is unarguably acknowledged as the leading light of medical imaging in India. Professor Sneh Bhargava trained in Delhi and rapidly went on to set standards for herself and the nation in the field of medical services. In a career that is even today nowhere close to sundown, she has displayed the pioneering spirit, the spirit of public service and the zeal for innovation that few can match. Persistence and dedication during her tenures as chief of radiodiagnosis and imaging and then as director of AIIMS, New Delhi, saw her realize her vision of bringing world-class technology to the poorest Indian.

Her systematic and meticulous approach to modern-day teaching and the practice of radiology and imaging continues to pay large dividends to the patients and clinicians she serves. Her fascination for the latest in technology blends harmoniously with her belief that if a task needs to be done, it will be done. It is these qualities that are sought in the speaker who is awarded this oration. She continues to inspire, train and administer in a style all her own, a style that is the essence of a bright future for India. A style worth emulating for administrators, physicians and doctors. We thank the Almighty to have brought us under her wing and to have given us wings.

Saru Bhartia
Deputy Director, Sitaram Bhartia Institute of Science and Research

In early 2008, Abhishek and I decided to take a sabbatical and leave for Boston to study for a year. The first question we had in mind was – 'Who would take charge of the hospital in our absence?' After reviewing all the options, we decided to request Dr Sneh Bhargava to take the position of the medical director while we were away. She graciously accepted the position and took charge. During these times, she was in charge of the overall functioning of the hospital. In our absence but under her leadership, the hospital ran smoothly. When we came back, Abhishek asked her to continue in her position.

Upon my return I had the opportunity to work with Dr Bhargava closely. I saw her come to work immaculately dressed in a sari with a different brooch every day. She would come in wearing her white coat and be ready to take the hospital round unless there was any urgent matter to address. On her hospital round, she would go to every patient room, every hospital department and talk to patients and staff and hear their concerns. This was a sight to behold. A petite five foot, 80-year-old woman with white, shiny hair and the energy of a 40-year old, doing her round, with housekeeping, maintenance and nursing managers bringing up the rear. As she did her round, she would leave behind a stillness in the air from the areas she had passed. Anyone passing through the same area a little later would know that she just been there. Absolutely everybody was scared of her but respected her.

Immediately after the rounds, she would sit down with the entire team and review and try to resolve every single issue raised by patients and staff. That is how she would start her day at Sitaram Bhartia. Each day, every day, without fail.

As I worked closely with her, I saw that she was open to new ideas and ready to review the latest ones and work for long hours. There were times when we would go from one meeting to the other, and I would have to remind her that it was lunchtime and we could stop but she insisted on finishing the meetings first. Under her leadership we first applied for accreditation by the National Accreditation Board for Hospitals and Healthcare Providers in 2014. She led from the front. Before we applied for the accreditation, we spent six months preparing for it. She read the Board's manual cover to cover and then had individual meetings with all the concerned stakeholders. She reviewed each department manual and the apex manual page by page. For days to come, she sat for hours with the manuals and reviewed them to get everything perfect. On the days of assessment, she was there from the time the assessors walked into the hospital to the time she saw them off and everything in between.

There were times when I would be with her in meetings and saw how she treated people. From a security guard to a middle-level manager, from a senior surgeon to a senior politician, she knew how to communicate with each of them. She is a no-nonsense person but never disrespectful. Once, a patient's attendant walked into her chamber and started complaining. She listened to him patiently until he questioned the ethics of the hospital. This is when her manner changed and she took him to task. She took a firm stance on the hospital's ethics and integrity, stressing the importance of those values to her and the institution. The attendant was taken aback. He had not expected such an assertive and energetic response from someone of her age. He realized his mistake later and apologized for his behaviour.

Of the many things I learnt from her, integrity was at the top of the list. She taught me that procrastination had no place in management and there was no substitute for hard work. She lives and stands by her values.

Dr Bhargava is also more than a great doctor and administrator. She enjoys a rich and varied life beyond her professional commitments. Besides work, she loved to travel, do gardening and make jam. She had an active social life. I used to wait to see her all dressed up on Saturdays for her kitty party. Whenever we have gone out for lunch or dinner, people have always come up and introduced themselves as her students or patients. She is an impeccable host and a family person.

Behind her desk are innumerable awards – national and international – that are too numerous to fit onto the wall. Dr Bhargava is truly a remarkable blend of professional success and personal fulfilment. I feel fortunate to have known her.

PB-24332
आ/5/उ